How to Beat The Blahs

by

Arnold Prater

Scripture quotations marked NASB are from the NEW AMERICAN STANDARD BIBLE, © The Lockman Foundation 1960, 1962, 1963, 1968, 1971, 1972, 1973, 1975, and are used by permission.

Scripture quotations marked RSV are from the REVISED STANDARD VERSION of the Bible, copyrighted 1946, 1952 © 1971, 1973. Used by permission.

Scripture quotations marked TLB are from THE LIVING BIBLE, copyright 1971, Tyndale House Publishers, Wheaton, Illinois. Used by permission.

HOW TO BEAT THE BLAHS

Irvine, California 92714
Library of Congress Catalog Card Number: 77-24827
ISBN 0-89081-038-9

Printed in the United States of America

Introduction

Ups and downs, joys and sorrows, happiness and saddness, excitement and boredom . . . this is life! . . . However, anyone of these emotions could cause you to have a miserable, unhappy feeling. The fizz and p-zaz evaporate from life. A big, grey cloud hangs overhead. Your heart feels as though you've had a transfusion of lead instead of blood . . . and you say . . . "I've got the blahs!"

We've all felt the blahs sometime in our life . . . maybe even right now you wonder: How do I get rid of the blahs? . . . In fact, why do I even have them? . . . How did they get started? NOW! . . . How do I beat them?

To answer these many questions, I would like to share with you from the things I have learned through my struggles, problems, needs and experiences in counseling. I have learned what makes people hurt and want to help them to "beat the blahs."

Arnold Prater

Contents

Chapter One

Forgive Us Our Offenses, Our Defenses and Our Pretenses!

God is not turned off by our humanity. He is turned off by our trying to cover it up! He is not turned off by what we are but by what we constantly pretend to be.

When Jesus let the Pharisees have it between the eyes it was not so much because of their deeds but their pretense. It was their whitewash that chilled our Master!

We know pretense is phony but somehow we still have the idea that if a Christian admits to being troubled, burdened, bowed down, or to having the blahs, there is something wrong with his discipleship.

Unconsciously we have been taught to think, "If I

really loved Christ, I'd never be in this condition. I'd never get upset, worry, have doubts or become discouraged. If I really loved Him, these things would not come into my life.''

Nonsense! That kind of thinking is an outright denial of our humanity and we are never more phony than when we try to do that!

On the night before He died Jesus said to His followers, ''Let not your hearts be troubled . . .'' (John 14:1, RSV). Now why would He say a thing like that unless He knew that they were going to have hearts that *were* troubled? He knew there would be times when His followers would be dogged by the blahs.

When your best friend lets you down, how are you, as a Christian, supposed to react? Should you sing ''Jesus wants me for a sunbeam''? No, such a thing hurts, stabs and bleeds. It gives you a very faint idea of what Jesus went through on the cross.

But if that is too easy try this one on. Your loved one is taken from you suddenly, instantly, out of the blue, in a flash. How are you supposed to react? As if it were really an inconsequential thing, since we are going to live forever anyhow?

If you try and force that attitude onto your broken heart you will never be more untrue to your humanity. Even Jesus wept before the tomb. Besides, there are tears of victory, and those kind are always a mixture of exquisite pain and joy.

So when Jesus said to His followers, ''Let not your hearts be troubled,'' He was acknowledging that they would be battling troubled hearts the rest of their days.

It is not *from* trouble that Jesus delivers us, it is *in* trouble! Picture the scene in which He said, ''Let not your hearts be troubled.''

It was late at night. One of His followers had slipped away and sold Him out. Even then the Roman soldiers were assembling for the arrest march. The plans for his death were complete. The trial was to be a farce, a mob would assemble and put unbearable pressure on the governor. Jesus was a doomed man about to suffer a most horrible death. It was the last night of His life.

It was on *that* night that He said, ''Let not your hearts be troubled . . .'' And through His Word that has lived through the centuries He is still saying it to us today!

He was about to die, but He wasn't pretending that everything was lovely. He was acknowledging the rough times that are stitched into the garments of life. He was facing up to the reality of tribulations. He said . . ''In the world you have tribulation; but be of good cheer, I have overcome the world'' (John 16:33, RSV).

This is a firm affirmation of His complete Lordship over every situation that can arise. Jesus is looking for frank faith, not frightened following! If I am His and I have given Him permission to live out His life in me using my mind and body, then He is in command of every situation that arises. Surely, that includes those times when I have the blahs.

WHY A BOOK ABOUT THE BLAHS?

I wrote this book for honest people who realize their hearts are troubled—that they have the blahs. You have been asking some honest questions and you want some honest answers. You've had enough of phoniness and self-deception.

You have come to this point in your life with some real needs. Life, as you have been living it, is not satisfying. Oh, you endure it and go through with it, but there is no sparkle, no fizz. The carbonation and thrill have gone out of it. For you, it is more like merely existing.

Perhaps there was a time when life was exciting, when you looked forward to each new day, when it was adventurous to love, laugh and plan. There was a time when you were excited about your faith.

What happened? Perhaps your mate was taken, the children are gone from the home, or the pace is too furious. Perhaps you live in a sour situation, or maybe you just got older and more stubborn and inflexible and stopped being teachable! Whatever it is, life has lost that sharp edge. But it doesn't have to be.

I don't believe the God Who made mountains and oceans, roses and lilies, little children and kittens meant for us to live life any other way than abundantly! Jesus said it Himself. He came so that His followers might ". . . have life, and have it abundantly" (John 10:10, RSV).

I was once a high school football coach. When we lost a game I learned that the thing to do was to correct mistakes we had made and the place to begin was with the fundamentals!

Some time ago I was walking down a long hall in the airport in a northern city. There was a billboard on the wall. Obviously it had been placed there by an advertising company that wished to sell the space. The words on it were these:

Three Tests For Good Ad Space

IS ANYBODY THERE?
IS ANYBODY LISTENING?
DOES ANYBODY CARE?

You seek an untroubled heart. You want to know how to handle the blahs. You want honest answers to honest questions, so we must begin with the fundamentals. I believe that those three tests for good ad space contain fundamental questions for all of us.

IS ANYBODY THERE?

Let's deal with them. Take that first one, is anybody there? Well, *is* there a God? Surely there is some kind of ongoing power behind the planets, galaxies and universes, which nobody in his right mind would deny. But a power behind the creation and a Supreme *Being* are two vastly different things. Is there *anybody* there? Is there a God, and especially is there a God who is *personal* and *loving*?

That's a fundamental. That's a basic. If the answer here is no, then nothing else really matters. If the answer is yes, then ultimately nothing else really matters!

Is there anybody there? Sometimes you have to wonder.

The millions of Jews who died under Hitler were no better and no worse than you and I. They did not deserve that kind of fate. As you look at the injustices and inequities in the world you can almost say, "Our universe is impartial. There is no God, at least not a personal God who takes an interest."

I was in a nursing home recently and there I saw a "body" containing a human person. That woman was a very small mass of human flesh with no arms, no legs and a tumor growing from one of her eyes. She had existed like this for over sixty years!

A friend of ours visited her physician and cancer was found. She was a beautiful young mother with two adorable children, just ready to start living.

I don't have to go on, you know what kind of a world it is. You know the pain, the sorrow, the heartbreak and suffering. Well, is anybody there? Is there a God? How can there be, when unfair things such as these exist?

It is just because of the undeserved tragedy and suffering there is in the world that I believe in God! Does that shock you? It shouldn't.

You see, if there is nobody there, if there is no God, then that can only mean one thing. That can only mean that evil, inequity, unfairness and injustice will ultimately triumph. Everything within me screams out its protest at this conclusion. I cannot believe it and neither can you!

The evil and suffering, the undeserved catastrophes, the injustice and the unfair things that happen to people—these are all arguments for God (not that He causes these things, heaven forbid!). They are arguments *for* everlasting life because they mean that some day the books will be balanced. Someday the righteous will be justified. Put simply it means that someday that precious little woman with no arms and no legs, with the eye tumor, will be set free. She will have a new body—one that is perfect. She will know the joy of walking into the sunset and stopping to cuddle the first rose of springtime!

The last name of God is Omega and that means He controls the end as well as the beginning. That's good news for anyone who cares to lend his mind and heart to what every fiber of his being tells him is true! All that is within us that is decent and noble and right universally protests that evil, inequity and injustice will not have the last word and be allowed to triumph.

The very presence of evil in the world is proof that there *is* Somebody there, that our faith in God has not been misplaced and that after this life, there is more!

IS ANYBODY LISTENING?

Yes, there is Somebody there, but does He *hear* us? Is anybody listening? Does He hear our cries?

Listening is a lost art, at least among people. Our land is full of people who are frantically seeking someone to listen. Some of us will pay seventy-five dollars an hour to a psychiatrist just for the purpose of finding a listener.

Ionesco strikingly illustrates this in one of his plays. Two people meet on a commuter train, a man and a woman. They get to talking and discover they live in the same apartment building. Then they discover each has a small daughter. Next they discover their apartment numbers are the same and finally they discover they are married!

A woman who had gone down the road from alcohol to hard drugs finally struck bottom. In my office she said to me, "I think I would have made it, if only once someone had looked at me as if I were *someone* instead of *something*!"

But does God listen? I believe He does because if He is there it follows that He is interested in our problems. If there is a God who guarantees with His only Son that evil and injustice shall not have the last word, could *that* kind of a God leave us, drop us down into this cybernetic, hopped-up, whirlpool of events and relationships and just leave us to sink or swim by ourselves? Not hardly. The old song has it right: "His heart is touched with my grief . . ." Deep down, with that indefinable faculty we cannot even name, much less define, we *know* that He listens!

If the books will be balanced at last, and if He is not too busy to attend even the funeral of a little sparrow that falls to the ground, *then God listens*.

We say we want honest answers to honest questions. Very well then, ask yourself this: Is anybody listening to *Him*? Is anybody listening to the answers He has for us?

That's getting a bit sticky, I know. Yet our rivers are polluted, our forests are gutted and our oxygen depleted. We've got national and international problems like we can't believe. We need answers, but is anyone listening for God's answers? Not many ever have and the tragic results are strewn across history.

He sent the prophets and they stoned them, threw them in prison and murdered them. He sent John the Baptist and they chopped off his head. He finally sent His only begotten Son and they dragged Him off to a dirty little mountain shaped like death itself and crucified Him. In every generation they have not listened.

But talking about "them" let's us off the hook. If we are interested in asking honest questions, surely we will permit one in return.

We come with a troubled heart, the blahs, but are we listening concerning the direction our lives should take from now on? Are we listening to God about what we ought to do with our time, our money, our talents?

Are we listening to God about what we ought to be doing to take care of our health? What is He saying to us about our marriage? About our relationships with our children, our church, with the people where we work? Are we listening to what He says about these things?

It is an outright cop-out to ask honest questions and look for honest answers unless we are ready to give some honest answers ourselves. So with that in mind let's hasten on to the third question that zapped my heart in that airport hallway.

DOES ANYBODY CARE?

Yes, there is a God, He listens, *but does He care?* Just to know that somebody cares is a basic need programmed into us all from the cradle to the grave.

If I sense I am unloved, I have in that moment laid the foundation for neurosis. Much personality damage springs from the root cause of lack of love.

Does God care? Please don't take my word for it. Let's go back to the Book for someone who has an indisputable right to give us an unequivocal answer.

Simon Peter was blessed by the Master. Jesus looked squarely into those flashing fisherman's eyes and told him that upon him He was going to build His eternal church (Matt. 16:13-18). Later, Peter was privileged to accompany the Lord Jesus to the top of the mountain and to feast on the splendors of the transfiguration vision (Matt. 17:1-8).

And after that, Peter had cursed and denied His Lord not once but three times in order to save his own neck, just as Jesus said he would. (Matt. 26:30-56)

But all that was forgiven and redeemed in the poignant scene on the shores of Galilee. Three times Jesus asked Peter, "Do you love Me?" Three times Peter answered "Yes," and each time Jesus gave him the same lifelong responsibility: "Feed by sheep." (John 21:15-19).

Later, when the Holy Spirit came upon the church at Pentecost, Peter became a rock as Jesus said he would. He obeyed Christ's command and "fed the sheep," showing thousands the way of salvation. (Acts 2-5.)

When he was an old, old man, Peter wrote these words in one of the epistles that bear his name: "Cast all your anxieties on Him, for He cares about you" (I Peter 5:7, RSV).

If anyone knew Jesus cares, Peter did.

George Newton is a turned-on layman from Fairbury, Nebraska. In a Sunday morning service they called for him to come forward and give a lay witness.

George came forward and stood silent for a long moment. Then he called for his wife. She came forward and he put his arm about her. Then slowly he turned and pointed to the chancel wall on which there hung a great cross. Utterly overcome and caught up in the awareness of the love of God and what He had done in his life, George pointed and simply said, "That Cross! . . . *That Cross*!"

Then he turned, and they slowly walked back to their

seats. He had said it all!

Does God care? Look once again yonder on that hill outside that ancient city where He hangs, suspended halfway between heaven and earth.

> "See from his head, his hands, his feet,
> Sorrow and love flow mingled down,
> Did e'er such love and sorrow meet,
> Or thorns compose so rich a crown?"

Does God care? That Cross! . . . *That Cross*! Could we invert that question once more? Let us be honest enough to do it. *Do we care?*

Do we really want honest answers? Do we really want the untroubled heart? Do we want to be changed by Christ because it is a sin to be small when we could be large, dwarfed when we could be giants? Or do we really seek justification for going on like we are, on the grounds that there are no truly honest answers?

There is the possibility that truth has been crucified in many of us long enough. There is the possibility that it is this condition of half-honesty that is keeping Christ from giving us His parting gift, the gift of the untroubled heart, the power and faith to handle the blahs.

A good friend of mine relayed this story to me. In Tennessee the local papers carried the story of how, on a cold and cloudy day, a local minister was found dead on a street corner in the city slums. Subsequent investigation revealed that he had gone early that morning to deliver medicine to a very poor family.

This last trip, just one of many he had taken over the years in behalf of desperate people, proved too much for his overburdened heart. There on the city streets among those he loved, the Lord decided he had finished his earthly task and called him home.

Then a wonderful thing happened. The physician who performed the autopsy pronounced the cause of death as "An overdose of living!"

Is your heart troubled? Do you have the blahs? Have you been somehow unable or unwilling to receive the gift our Lord says He has for us all?

If you are tired enough of being "dead," maybe you need to end that with an overdose of living!

It's this business of commitment which has to be settled before we begin to deal with the daily-living-blahs. When we have dealt with that, then we'll be ready to deal with these other things.

Settle that and, I promise, you'll go on a discovery voyage that can be exciting, thrilling and life-changing!

Hurry now, don't keep Him waiting!

Chapter Two

All the Things That Bug Us Do Not Fly!

The only difference between the word "blah" and "hallelujah" is Jesus Christ.

Now that you have upgraded your commitment, we are ready to go on. I don't think I have to go into detail about the blahs. We all have them, those kind of days when we should have stayed in bed. Everything just seems to shift into gray and no matter what we start to do it turns out wrong. You're with me, aren't you? I'm speaking of the daily-living blahs.

King David knew what it was to have the blahs, to be depressed. You don't steal another man's wife, send him to his death and lose your young son to disease without ending up in some dark valleys. In seminary they tried to teach me that the twenty-third Psalm is a "pastoral" psalm. One is supposed to form mental pictures of frolicking sheep, tranquil days, the shepherd's soft, sweet flutes and that sort of thing. I don't believe it for a minute!

I believe that life finally served up its bill to David. He descended into the valley of the shadows of sickness, depression, sin and death and there, in spite of his kingly authority, the enormity of his need and his own personal inadequacy engulfed him completely.

Down there in that lowest of low valleys he made the glorious discovery that even there the Lord God, his heavenly Father, was with him. Because of his Lord no evil could ultimately touch him. God was not defeated by anything, even sin and death, and David realized he could have victory!

I believe that David threw back his head and shouted "Glory to God!" Then he began to write: "The Lord is my Shepherd . . . I shall not want!" Thrills of victory —a mixture of pain and joy—swept over him as he made discovery after discovery that he need not fear evil, that his enemies were helpless, that the table was prepared. The anointing horn, filled with the oil of the power of God, was poised and ready.

I believe when David wrote *that* Psalm, he was shouting, clapping his hands and jumping for joy. He finally *knew* that he didn't have to go it alone. God's goodness and mercy were his boon companions from here on in! (Why don't you just stop for a moment and thank Him a while, yourself!)

There are four words in the twenty-third Psalm that give us the clue as to how Jesus Christ delivers us from the troubled heart of discouragement: "He restores my soul . . . ."

I don't think it damages the text one bit if you see Jesus as the Great Restorer. He is the Great Shepherd, the leader into green pastures, the guide back from the storm to the still waters. He is the One who goes before us into the valley of the shadow of death, down there where there is darkness, despair and heartbreak and Who leads us back out into the light again.

Well, how does He do it? You've got the blahs for one reason or another and you believe that Jesus Christ is the Great Restorer, but what does that *mean* in all meat-and-potatoes practicality?

UPS AND DOWNS ARE PART OF LIFE

One thing to realize is that it's a perfectly "normal" thing for you and me to have cycles in our lives. We live life like the graph lines on an electrocardiogram. There are slow peaks and sudden valleys. There are sudden peaks and slow valleys. Things are never level for very long.

We know this, but it is still tough for us to accept the fact that we cannot live on Cloud Nine all the time. For example, when Peter, James and John were with Him on the mount of Great Joy they wanted to remain there and just have praise services from then on. They wanted to stay and sing and praise and witness, but He took them back down to face the challenges of the valley, where in no time at all they were faced with the blahs. (Matt. 17:1-21.)

We are human (and therefore imperfect) and so we get the blahs. The glow doesn't last. We think God has deserted us, or that we have deserted Him.

Sometimes we want to deny our humanity and refuse to accept the reality of the valley, but that is unreal. It's phony. To pretend ecstasy is sometimes bad, but to pretend religious ecstasy is *always* bad!

Our problem is that we have had it pounded into us that the only time we love God is when we are having spiritual highs.

There is no thrill like being caught up in praise and adoration, there is no thrill like being "turned on" in the name of Christ. But an even greater thrill is to discover we can love God when we are in the midst of spiritual lows!

The Bible tries to show us this. Read again the story of Elijah and how he put to shame several hundred priests of Baal on the mountaintop in view of the great assembly. You remember how the priests of Baal called on their god to consume the offering on the altar, but nothing happened. Then Elijah called on Jehovah and his God sent fire that consumed the offering. It was a great victory for Elijah—a spiritual high.

Soon, however, evil Queen Jezebel heard about Elijah's triumph and vowed to kill him. When Elijah, the mighty prophet, who the day before had soared high in triumph, heard about her threats, he panicked. He ran off into the desert, sat down under a tree and took a spiritual bubble bath in an ocean of self-pity! He was so depressed he said, "It is enough; now, O Lord, take away my life!" (I Kings 19:1-4, RSV.)

Up one minute, down the next! Welcome to the human family, Elijah, O mighty man of God!

Here's still another example of a giant who didn't always feel that triumphant. Charles Wesley, who joined his brother, John, as one of the great evangelists of the 18th century, wrote "O For a Thousand Tongues to Sing"—a spiritually high hymn if there ever was one. But, less than a year after his remarkable conversion to Christ, Wesley sat down one gloomy day and wrote another hymn. It's title? "O Where Is the Blessedness I Knew When First I Met the Lord?"

Charles Wesley also knew what they were like—the blahs!

When *will* we face up to the fact of our humanity and see that we are not made to live on the mountain all the time. Besides, there is very little growth up there above the timberline. The thin, heady air is not conducive to it. The view is great but the real growth takes place in the valley, where the air is heavy, where the wind and rain and storms occur. Where the lightning releases nitrogen into the soil.

We cannot go through life like super-angels, inwardly aflame, insulin flowing, thirsting every moment after the souls of persons lost from God. There are times when we can do it, but if we try to stretch it too far we soon begin to pretend and then it becomes phony.

We are cyclical creatures. God doesn't mind when we sometimes have to descend. He made us that way. And sometimes we *do* have to descend.

We have to wash socks and underwear, fix leaky faucets, iron clothes, pay bills. We must write letters, mow lawns and earn a living. We seem to have the necessity occasionally to have colds, fever, acid indigestion, throbbing sinuses, backaches, runny noses, and upset stomachs. If we didn't, how could the TV commercial writers survive?

We simply do not always have to be *doing* something

for God. Much as we may hate to admit it He will not go out of business if we slow down, or lose a bit of our zeal for a while.

Sometimes, like our Lord Jesus, we have to lie down in the boat and sleep in the very midst of the storm, serene in the confidence that God can run the world. He will awaken us and call us when He has something special for us to do.

One dear, sweet friend of mine wrote me, "Sometimes I get so tired and frustrated, I just have to stop and be His!" Isn't that great? Try it sometime soon. Just stop all the rushing and fretting and "be His."

FROM DESCENDING TO DEPENDING

"He restores our souls . . ." but to *what* does He restore us? Back to the mountaintop? Sometimes, but more often than not He restores us from *descending to depending*. He gives us the power to descend. As we depend on Him, we receive grace for the letdowns. We gain inner resources for the bad days—the blahs.

Not long ago I paid a visit down into the valley. I had just been in a great, thrilling, exciting Christian meeting. Wonderful things had happened. People had found Christ for their lives, marriages straightened out, problems were met, needs were satisfied by Him. All in all, it was terrific!

I went home, fell straight down off the mountain and never stopped my descent until I hit bottom. I sat there in kind of a spiritual stupor (remember Elijah?). The fizz went out of the days and the joy leaked away and I literally cried out, "O God, what happened? Where are you?"

Of course He came. He always does, not to take me back up on the mountain but to teach me something I desperately needed to learn, the same thing He taught Elijah. If you know the story you know that God came to Elijah there in that wilderness of discouragement and spoke in a still, small voice. (I Kings 19:9-18.)

That's how the Holy Spirit came to me and quietly made me aware of how subtly, deep down, without verbalizing it, I was taking credit for the victories of the past week. I had straightened out the homes and marriages and given those souls rebirth. It was *my* talent which had brought these grand things to pass.

Oh, I hadn't said it, but I had thought it, savored it and glowed in self-satisfaction. I had the quiet bighead and it stopped up my glory-valve! It always does!

After I had humbly asked His forgiveness He restored my soul, from descending to depending. I know that without Him I cannot make it. I cannot manage my own life for even one hour a day. So every hour on the hour I have to give it all to His Lordship. Sometimes on the half-hour!

I often wonder why I have to learn it over and over. I tire of having to relearn everything, but He does not tire of having to re-teach me, because He knows what He wants to make out of me. He keeps His eye on the end product while I can only see the present moments. He is not going to be sidetracked. He is going to hold my nose to the learning stone!

Next time you fall off of your mountain, take a long hard look backwards. More often than not it is an ego problem. A prayer was answered, a victory won, a task accomplished and you didn't thank Him. You were not really grateful. Oh, you nodded at Him as you savored the triumph but your heart wasn't in it. You got what you wanted, you had it your way. Then subtly, oh so very subtly, you took the credit. Next thing you knew you had the blahs.

But in a way, when you get the blahs, it's a perfect time to praise God. The twenty-third Psalm says, "He makes me lie down . . ." Could it be He allows me to get the blahs so I can be reminded of how helpless I really am? There are times when I feel sure the Lord has made me lie down by giving me the blahs. Then, and only then, He can lead me to the green pastures.

FROM FRETTING TO FAITH

Jesus is the Great Restorer. Here is another thing I have found. He restores me from *fretting to faith!*

Fretting is a great symptom of the troubled heart, the blahs. Here we are, rescued for eternity by what Jesus Christ has done for us, and committed by Him into the loving hands of our heavenly Father. He it was, who held in His hands the flaming mass and pounded out on the anvil of His divine will the creation and all that is in it. We are held and kept safe in the hands of *that* God. But still we fret and stew ourselves into the boiling pots of outright anxiety and life's sweetness is soon cooked away!

I heard a woman say the other day the only thing still holding her together was her hair spray!

We like to tell ourselves "rational lies." We say that our fretting is only "normal concern" or something like that, but the hard truth is that our fretting is a fairly accurate reflection of just how truly self-centered we really are.

For when we strip away the outer wrapping from our fretting the truth is revealed. The reason we fret is because we want our own way, regardless. We are desperately concerned that things turn out the way *we* want. It reveals how utterly uncompromising we are in our notions about how our lives should run and what the end results should be.

Just make a list of the things you commonly fret about and see if this is not true. Your children. Are you really concerned that this thing you are fretting about in their lives turns out for their ultimate benefit or that everything be solved and finalized in the pattern you have cut out?

Fretting and possessiveness live on the same side of the tracks. We fret about money, popularity, clothes, food, housing, the church, the pastor, taxes, crops, fellow workers, the government, cars, status. The list is endless, but the application is the same.

Or we crank up the old imagination, which is the pad from which the missiles of fretting are usually launched. Junior has the car tonight for the first time. We sit at home and think about it. We know it is one of the things we must accept, but soon smoke curls up from the launching pad, the missile is ignited and blasts off. We see Junior driving too fast, there is a curve, the crash, the telephone rings, the ambulance, the hospital and finally we imagine Junior in the funeral parlor itself.

Actually, Junior has not gotten three blocks down the street and is happily on his way. Meanwhile, we are frazzled, dazzled, razzled and completely, absolutely, unequivocally unglued!

If there was any one thing our Lord Jesus was not, He was not a fretter. He was not obsessed with making things turn out His way. He was concerned that things turn out God's way, because He knew that nothing that happened could ultimately defeat God. When you really believe *that*, you can be nailed to a cross and still march away from it in triumph!

Jesus committed each day, each hour and each circumstance as it arose into God's hands.

Fortunately God is not turned off by our failures and by our humanity. If He thought we were worth dying for, He surely thinks we are worth teaching. That is why Jesus constantly restores us from fretting to faith.

So David exulted "He restoreth my soul . . . ." but how? Well, again, He usually does not do it in one great blinding moment accompanied by lightning and thunder. He does not surgically remove from us the *capacity* to fret. He respects our personhood too much to do that.

He simply brings us down out of orbit and gives us reentry by His Holy Spirit. He motivates us to stop fretting and insisting on our own way in *this* circumstance. He heals our blindness until we *see* that to trust Him for the outcome in *this* circumstance is all that is required for now.

There will always be another day, another circumstance and another now. God had to work this process in Paul time and time again until finally Paul began to get the point. One day he sat down and wrote, "We *know* that in everything God works for good with those who love Him . . ." (Romans 8:28, RSV, italics mine).

Every day you may win some and lose some, but you never finish playing life's ball games. There are more to be played tomorrow, and in all of the tomorrows to come, until faith becomes sight and sight becomes knowledge.

All I know for now is that He restores my soul from fretting to faith and that I cannot do it myself!

FROM JUDGMENT TO JOY

In order to deliver us from the blahs and bless us with the untroubled heart Jesus restores us from descending to depending, from fretting to faith, and I have found still another thing. He restores us from *judgment to joy!*

If there is any one thing from which we need to be restored it is our seemingly constant need to play God! Of sitting in judgment on other people.

Of all the roadblocks to Christian joy, being judgmental is one of the most formidable!

Restoration at this point comes from being able to see people through the eyes of Christ. When I am looking at people through His eyes, I do not judge them unfairly because I see them with His love. When I see them through human eyes, my own, I see them through a filter of fears, hostilities and anxieties and that is not the soil of love.

When we see people out of our own eyes we demand and expect an acceptable performance. The fact that *we* don't perform properly, and that we expect others to perform not properly but perfectly, only shows the impossibility of loving human relationships without Jesus Christ.

When people don't measure up to our expectations and demands we chew them up and spit them out. We cut and slash them to ribbons. It is the cruelest form of punishment there is, and it happens because one human refuses to let another *be human!*

That is what happens when we look at people through human eyes. Besides, we always look at the wrong things. For example, what we look at is bodies. Handsome people with beautiful bodies turn us on. Ugly people with ugly bodies turn us off.

We are conditioned this way. I remember the nicknames we gave one another when we were children. There was a boy in our class who always had his head shaved, so we called him "Cleanhead." "Hey, Cleanhead, let's play ball."

There was another who had a bad overbite, we called him "Bottle Opener." "Hey, Bottle Opener, whatcha doin'?" There was still another who only had one eye. We called him "Single-Barrel!" Their nicknames were all body associated.

Jesus was not distracted by the bodies of people unless they stood in need of healing. Jesus always looked at spirits instead of bodies.

If we saw people through Christ's eyes we would do the same. In that case, Miss America could be blind and clubfooted and it wouldn't matter.

If we practiced seeing people through Christ's eyes He would restore us from judgment to joy. We could see that many times beautiful bodies house miserable, dried up spirits and unattractive bodies provide homes for spirits breathtakingly beautiful.

When beautiful bodies house beautiful spirits it is a glorious thing. Far more glorious, however, is accepting persons *as they are.* When we are judgmental, demanding and demeaning we have a guaranteed formula for living constantly with hearts that are troubled—the blahs.

If your heart is troubled today, if you have the blahs, is it because you have been looking at somebody through your own eyes? Have you been demanding levels of acceptability they cannot produce? Have you been looking at bodies rather than spirits?

There is a grand woman I know in a deep south state who had a stroke years ago. She is crippled and twisted and bent and speaks with a pitiful quaver in her voice that is almost unbearable. Her mouth is deeply drawn to one side and the saliva constantly dripping from it causes one to want to run away.

But if you deny that impulse and look down into her soul past that stricken body, you see shining up from the depths a pool of unspeakable beauty that must cause the very angels of heaven to gasp with delight.

And when you hear the spirit behind that drooling, quavering mouth as she says, "God is so wonderful . . . and good . . . to me . . ." it is almost more joy than you can bear!

Jesus restores us from judgment to joy, but it takes time. He seldom does it all at once in some cataclysmic experience that instantly and forever rids us of all our hang-ups and prejudices toward people. He does it from person-to-person, from situation to situation, and one day at a time.

As you come into new situations and into the lives of people just simply ask Christ to give you His eyes.

If He gave His whole body for us upon Calvary's cross . . . will He not give us His eyes if we ask? Yes, He will. I know that He will.

But we may only use them for one person at a time,

one situation at a time and one day at a time.

Someone came into the room where Pablo Casals, the famous musician, was practicing. His visitor was utterly astounded to see him practicing the scales on the cello.

"Why are you bothering to spend your time with something so simple as the scales?" the visitor asked.

"Because," Casals said, "the problem in playing the cello lies in getting from one note to the next. That is why I must always be practicing the scales!"

Jesus Christ lends us His eyes for one person at a time, one situation at a time and one day at a time. Our problem is in getting from one challenge to the next. It's up to us to be constantly practicing our scales!

Chapter Three

Discipleship Is What You Do After You Say, "I Believe!"

The other day I was strolling through God's Word and I found a diamond! I stooped over and picked it up, and I have been carrying it around, scarcely able to wait until I came to the proper place in which to share it with you. I had read it many times before but never in the New English Bible. "Peace is my parting gift to you, my own peace such as the world cannot give. Set your troubled hearts at rest and banish your fears." (John 14:27, NEB.)

God is offering us the gift of His peace. A gift is never forced on one. We must simply receive it. That is the only way to "set our troubled hearts at rest." It is the only way to handle the blahs.

It all sounds so simple, doesn't it? But alas, we know it is definitely *not* simple. At any rate, it is not easy. Evil is on the job and has an arsenal of weapons to constantly use on us.

There are those who do a great disservice by oversimplifying Christian discipleship. They will say, "It's so simple. Jesus Christ offers you the gift of His peace as the answer to a troubled heart. Well, if it is a gift, then we just take it by faith!"

We hear them and it sounds good and we *try*. But we know what happens, don't we? We soon wilt and the whole thing fizzles out. We beat our breasts and hang our heads and wonder what happened.

So back we go to those who told us to take it by faith and we tell them what happened. And they always have an irrefutable answer, "You didn't have *enough* faith!"

It's as if faith is something you can whip up by flipping your Faith Switch to "on." But if faith itself is a gift of God, how in the name of heaven can *we* turn it on?

Sometimes the most damnable thing that can be said to a desperate person is "You must not have had enough faith!"

Now let's reason through this. If faith is of God and if God is always more willing to give than we are to receive, then why does the way to God get blocked? More often than not it must be because of a *condition* in our lives rather than our lack of five gallons of faith, or seven gallons or whatever is supposed to be "enough."

Well, just what are some of these conditions which thwart and block God? I am sure there are many, but here are a few about which I can claim to be an authority simply because I have had so many bloody battles with them along the way. They frequently come buzzing in like hungry mosquitos and bury their beaks in my soul, resulting in king-sized blah-welts!

EVER HAD THE "WHEN I'S"?

Jesus had trouble with the "when I" kind of people. One day He called one of them to be His disciple and this fellow said, in effect, "All right, Master, *when I* say good-bye to those at home then I will come and follow you!"

Jesus rejected his excuse and said, "No one who puts his hand to the plow and looks back is fit for the kingdom of God" (Luke 9:62, RSV).

Now He did not say this out of an unfeeling heart. It wasn't because He had no compassion for the man in his grief. We know better than that. If He could weep before the tomb of Lazarus, then He cared about the sorrow of this man.

Jesus was trying to get our priorities straight. He was making the point that no *circumstance* offers a valid reason for rejecting the invitation to discipleship. No circumstance should shut off joy and inner assurance.

As far as we know this man couldn't see it. He went sadly away, buried his father and never did become a disciple of Jesus. It is significant that even his name is lost to us forever.

The "When I's."

When Paul was arrested and brought before the governor Felix, he testified and preached to him. He clearly pointed out the impossibility of salvation by good works and somehow Felix knew Paul was right. There was not a single argument with which to respond. Down deep, where it mattered most, the Spirit had made it plain that he had to make a decision, but he said, "Go away for the present; *when I* have an opportunity I will summon you" (Acts 24:25, RSV).

But, of course, after that Felix stayed out of the kitchen because he couldn't stand the heat!!!

There is a man in a certain city who earns $200,000 a year. His son has made a wreck of his life. His wife is bored and unhappy. This man has sold out to materialism and concluded it is the ultimate reality.

This man has a good Christian friend and one day he told him, "Some day I'm gonna change my life and hit this Christianity thing like you do and *when I* do . . . I'm gonna go all out!"

I know in my heart he means it, but the days are hastening by and he shows no signs of being "ready." So his life flows on, sapping meaning from each day and leaving him each evening with a troubled heart, the blahs.

The "When I's."

But let's make the Bible our model. Let's look at the elder brother of the Prodigal Son, standing sulking in the shadows, his ego shattered by all this fuss over his lost, vagrant brother. Inside, the great party is going on. There is music and laughter and joy because he who was dead is alive again, he who was lost is found.

We can hear the elder brother's father as he slips outside and begs him to come in where the rejoicing is taking place. But he shakes his head and though it is not recorded we can hear him saying, "*When I* have the calf killed in honor of *my* faithfulness, then I'll come inside with the rest!"

I remember a meeting at which I spoke many years ago in a small rural church. There was a man and his wife who had lived with troubled hearts for years. As far as I knew they had no place for God in their lives. But one night she heard the trumpet call from heaven in her heart and it showed on her face.

The next day I went to talk with her and what she said still haunts me to this day. "You're right. I'm ready to give whatever is left of my life to God, but I'm waiting for my husband. *When I* can talk him into it, we'll come and make our commitment."

But that has been years ago and like Felix of old, the more convenient time never arrived.

I remember another young man who said to me, "Now don't press me . . . I will make this decision *when I* feel like it, but I cannot be pressed!"

He was right, he couldn't. I watched his family disintegrate until it was divided and destroyed, but he never felt like giving up his troubled heart.

"*When I* feel like it."

There is a picture in my head of a man out in the woods. It is a clear, cold winter morning, and he is standing out there leaning on his axe. I walk up to him and say, "Good morning, friend, what are you going to do with that axe?"

And he answers, "I'm going to cut that tree down." And I reply, "Well, it's cold, why don't you get started?"

"I'm waiting until I begin to sweat!"

"But you're never going to sweat standing there in the cold like that!"

"It doesn't matter, I'm not going to swing this axe once until I start to sweat!"

That is so ridiculous that it is hardly worth a comment, but it's no more ridiculous than we are sometimes . . . waiting for some kind of mysterious religious feeling that never comes.

WHAT ARE YOUR "WHEN I'S"?

There are all kinds of "When I's" that spawn the blahs. When I get the children through college. When I get my bills paid, when I get settled down, when I get back from my trip, when I get that promotion, when I lose fifteen pounds, when interest rates drop, when I find the right church, when I get all my questions answered and on and on!

Meanwhile I'll just go on carrying this troubled heart inside and wondering why I have it. I'll go on being shut out of the abundant life, smothered by the ruthless, rigorous rote of routine religion. I'll keep on waiting, waiting, waiting, never facing up to the fact that I'd rather have a safe God on my leash doing my thing, when I know He would have me in His care, freed to do *His thing*!

It's so much easier just to go on being respected instead of being transformed!

Back to our model again. The Bible illustrates over and over again how yielding frees God to give the gift of the untroubled heart.

Jeremiah said, "Lord, I'm too young, when I get older I'll go!"

But God said, "The Syrians are outside the city, son, *get going*!"

Moses said, "Lord, I stutter and stammer. *When I* finish my speech therapy classes, I'll go!"

But God said, "My people are perishing, Moses, *go now*!"

David said, "Lord, I'm just a little, runny-nosed kid, *when I* grow up a bit, I'll go!"

But God said, "Boy, go fetch your slingshot, the giant is out there *now*!"

Jonah said, "*When I* get back from Tarsus, I'll go!"

But God said, "But Nineveh is about to be destroyed now, *so go*!"

What is that great problem in your life that has been standing like a flaming angel between you and paradise? What is that need you have, or that sour situation in which you're involved. What is that habit you've been going to break or that dreaded decision you've been waiting to make? What is there in your marriage you've been going to deal with but "not just yet"?

If we know anything at all about God's word we know it teaches us that He will never deal with us on our own terms in our own good times. He loves us too much to do that.

Life is not like some great huge storehouse bulging with an endless supply of time out of which flows a stream for us to spend and waste carelessly forever. Instead, life is an hourglass filled with just enough time for one brief lifetime, and it flows in a steady stream each day.

When each night falls, that day is spent forever. Deep down we know that God is not arbitrarily withholding the gift of His peace. When He calls us to some mission, He wants our response now!

HOW ABOUT THE "WHAT IF'S"?

Again, speaking as an authority only because I am frequently one of the chief transgressors, let me mention a second condition that prevents God's gift from being bestowed. If there could be anything worse than the "when I's" it has to be the "what if's!"

What if I get cancer? What if I have a heart attack? What if I lose my job? What if we use up our savings? What if I become an invalid? What if my daughter gets pregnant? What if we have another war? What if my son gets on drugs? What if the government goes broke?

And so the great cacophony of fear, gloom and pessimism and doubt arises to the ears of an omnipotent and all-powerful God. And all this whining says to Him, "We simply *cannot* trust you, God. These things are too big and too much for you. We know you can create and operate a hundred million universes and a hundred million galaxies, but these big problems and possibilities in *our* lives are too much for you. You have finally met your match!"

So the untroubled heart begins to send out symptoms of spiritual angina. Soon there's a mild case of spiritual cardiac arrest, a troubled heart—the blahs.

The Bible plainly illustrates the folly of the "what if's." The disciples said to Jesus, "Don't go down there to Jerusalem . . . it's a bad time. The authorities are upset. What if you lose your life?"

And Jesus said, "No you don't. I am not falling for that one . . . I must do the will of Him that sent me!" And He set His face to go to Jerusalem.

Or look at Peter, walking on the water toward the Lord. Suddenly he was seized by a case of the what if's!

"What if I should sink?" And the instant the negative, untrusting thought entered his mind he began to sink. It always happens when we allow the negative to take over.

Suppose Noah, when he was almost finished with the ark, had said, "What if I was imagining things? What if I didn't hear God's voice? What if it doesn't rain after all?"

If Noah had said that, he would have been the wettest carpenter this side of the Euphrates river!

Look at Gideon, his great army sliced down to three hundred men. Suppose he had said, "What if God can't handle this?"

What about Elijah, one man against four hundred and fifty priests of Baal, Samson against ten thousand Philistines or Daniel in the den with forty fasting lions? And we think we've got problems!!!

We have to come smack down to the crux of the matter, which is simply this: *God is trustworthy or He is not*! We are given the choice. We can trust Him or we can doubt Him. The untroubled heart always lies on the right side of the valley that divides fear and trust.

But then the voices begin. "To live life on this basis is risky . . . what if I lose my friends, my prestige, my possessions?" That is one "what if" that may become reality. But we are promised that whoever gives up houses, land or family or friends in this life will gain a hundredfold and that's the understatement of the century!

The friends God has given me across this land number literally in the thousands, and they are the greatest and finest people one can possibly imagine.

I emptied a lot of dirt out of my pockets and God filled

them up with diamonds. Since then I have been hard put to call that sacrifice!

Very near the top of the heap is the king-sized "What if" that proclaims "What if I can't handle it?"

If by that you mean you cannot live a perfect life, of course you can't. That is why we are rescued at last by God's matchless grace, not because we finally brought home a moral report card all marked with A's.

Our chief reason for living is to try to live and love more like Christ, but our salvation does not depend upon our Christlikeness. Our salvation depends upon Christ's *Godlikeness*, and two thousand years ago on that Roman cross out on that desolate hill He passed the test with flying colors!

Let me say again what was said in the beginning. I am not dealing primarily with our "eternal salvation." I am concentrating on our Christian struggle for Christlikeness in this segment of eternity called the now. Whether or not we enter heaven does not depend upon our degree of success. Through Christ we *shall* enter heaven, and our degree of success only determines the state in which we enter it.

THE BIGGEST "WHAT IF" OF THEM ALL

I have left the king-sized "What if" of them all until the last and it's this: "What if I don't have enough faith to see me through?"

Well, it may surprise you but I am glad God doesn't give us enough faith to see us through when we first turn to Him. Here's why.

Back in the days of passenger trains and steam locomotives, if you had gone with me down to the

Union Station in St. Louis, we could have walked up to the engine that pulled the train from St. Louis to Kansas City. We could have climbed up into the cab and looked it over. We could have seen the big steam gauge marked off to indicate a capacity for two hundred pounds of steam pressure. You could have noticed the needle stood at eighteen pounds.

Suddenly the conductor may have cried, "All Aboard!" The engineer would have eased the throttle back. That big drive shaft would have started to move, and the huge wheels to turn and you would have cried, "Wait a minute! It's almost three hundred miles to Kansas City, don't you know that? You surely can't be planning to go that far with only eighteen pounds of steam!"

The engineer would have smiled at you as he would have smiled at anyone who didn't know any more about steam engines than that. Those big wheels would have turned faster and faster until they were driving that train down the rails toward Kansas City at seventy miles per hour. The needle on that steam gauge would have crept higher and higher until it reached one hundred eight pounds. Then the engineer would have reached up and pulled that whistle cord right out in the open countryside. He would have let loose blast after blast on the whistle in order to empty steam from the boilers to keep them from exploding!

"What if I don't have enough faith to see me through?" God's way is to grant us all the faith we need, but He will only grant it one day at a time. All it takes to start is just a little faith the size of a grain of mustard seed!

If God gave us enough faith to see us through when

we start the Christian journey, we would just explode, defuse and defissionize. There wouldn't be anything left of us but split atoms, every one of them singing hallelujahs!

When the Bible promises that God shall supply all our needs, it means one day at a time. Read again the story of the manna in the wilderness. Tomorrow's supply is not due and collectable *until tomorrow*! It's the same with faith. When you have to have it most, that's when you'll always have the most of it!

Your need is what God will supply. He doesn't furnish any reserve tanks!

WHY NOT TRY THE "I WILL'S"?

We have already concluded that one doesn't handle the blahs by pulling one's faith switch and turning on an ample supply. We have seen that what hinders us is usually a condition. Two of those conditions are the "What I's" and the "What if's." We'll have to wait for heaven to find out which is the worst of the two.

If we want the way out of these two conditions we need to settle for the Biblical way, which is also a condition. But it is a positive one—the condition of the "I will's!"

The "When I's" and the "What if's" are only good for wallowing in weakness. The "I will's" release the power of God.

Again, to be on safe ground let us turn our attention to our model, the Word. Jeremiah said, "All right, Lord, I may be young, but *I will* go and warn against the Syrians!" When he said that, the vultures of doubt spread their great wings and flew off into outer darkness.

Moses said, "All right, even though I stutter and stammer, *I will* go down to Egypt and you can be my mouth and my speech!" And when he said that, his fear suffered a great stroke and fell quivering and paralyzed at his feet forevermore.

David said, "All right, Lord, I'm already down here picking up five smooth stones." And God said, "In that case you won't need but one stone."

Jonah said, "All right, Lord, I'm tearing up my ticket to Tarsus, I'll go to Nineveh!" And in the heart of Jonah, joy cracked like a sonic boom, shattering the shutters of his heart, and for the first time the light of peace poured in.

And under the olive branches of dark Gethsemane, when His sweat had become as great drops of blood falling to the ground, our Lord Jesus Christ said, "Nevertheless, not My will but Thine be done!"

When that happened, all the hallelujahs heaven had ever known joined hands and danced with everlasting joy around the throne of the Lord of heaven and earth!

God has given us one great and holy privilege and he would not let all the H-bombs of earth or the love-bombs of heaven interfere with it. It is our complete and absolute freedom to say, "I will!"

It is the one thing that binds us up or sets us free, for we can also say, "I won't."When we say "no" to God, we always say "yes" to something else!

Even after the battering ram of Christ's love has made a shambles of the door named Excuses, we can still say "no," but we need to remember that in that instant we have said "yes" to a troubled heart!

There in the pigpens at midnight in the far country,

the Prodigal Son could have said "no" to the call of his heart and "yes" to the pigpens. But after he finished with the "When I's" and the "What if's" he said, "*I will* arise and go to my father . . ." (Luke 15:18, RSV).

When he said that, all the lostness and despair in him broke into a thousand pieces, fell into the river of the Father's love and was carried away into the land of Nevermore. He began the journey back to the music, the laughter, the joy of the fatted calf and embrace of the father's loving arms.

We know we cannot do it in our own strength. But we also know that deliverance is as near as our own free will.

Once I knew of a little girl, long since gone to be with God. She had leukemia and had over two hundred blood transfusions. After each transfusion her temperature would go as high as 104 and she had to be packed in large quantities of ice.

But Janie was a radiant little Christian girl. One night she asked her daddy to explain what people meant by a "New Heart." He sat on the edge of her bed and tried to explain it. Like most fathers, he wasn't doing very well.

Suddenly Janie stopped. She laid her thin little hand on his and in a tiny voice she said, "Daddy, are you trying to say that what people must have . . . is a Jesus transfusion?"

Maybe that is more than can be said in an entire book, I don't know. That surely says it all.

Except that the gift of the untroubled heart only comes if we ask for it—only if we say, "I will!"

And when we do, the music begins in the Father's house!

Chapter Four

All Giants Don't Live at the Top of Beanstalks!

Not all people with problems are sick—it's how they deal with them that makes the difference.

In America we are trained to think that if we have a problem we *must* solve it. Sometimes, however, it may be better to learn how to *deal* with a problem than to get rid of it.

We know that as long as we inhabit bodies of flesh and blood and mix and mingle with people, as long as we are set loose in a world where there is disease, calamity and catastrophe, and as long as there is evil loose in that world, there are going to be constant attacks of the blahs. Our hearts are going to be troubled.

So it is sheer reality to focus on "handling" or dealing with our problems as they arise than to live in the vain hope that something is going to happen that will wipe them all out of existence from here on in.

That is precisely the reason we keep coming back to the Bible for our models. For the Christian, God is the Source and the Bible is the "Source Book." God speaks to us in many ways, but certainly the Bible is one of the chief media through which His loving Spirit reaches out to guide us.

The other day I had another attack of the blahs. They rolled in like an unexpected fog on the seashore, enveloping me. Sometimes there is nothing to do but wait until the fog begins to lift. Like driving in fog, we need to live very carefully until the fog begins to lift.

So when the fog began to lift I went again to the model for my answers on how to handle this particular type of attack. I went hungrily and receptively, and when we go to God's Word that way, we can be pretty sure He isn't going to turn us away.

This time I found my answers over in the Old Testament book of Numbers, in the thirteenth and fourteenth chapters.

Let me set the scene for you. The long journey was about to end. Moses had almost reached his goal. The Egyptians lay dead on the beaches behind them, the Red Sea was a problem that had been handled. The hunger of the people during the journey had been satisfied, for God had sent the manna to be gathered one day at a time, and what a lesson there was in that! God would care for them, *but only as their need arose*. He loved them too much to make them secure for longer than that, so when the people tried to store up the manna, it spoiled.

When the people complained about the monotony of the manna, God sent them meat. Thousands of quail came into the camp and their needs were met.

But now they stood on the very banks of the Jordan and across it lay Canaan, the promised land. So they made camp and God gave Moses his instructions. He was to select twelve spies, one from each of the tribes, send them into the land and have them look it over. Then they would come back and report.

The spies went into Canaan for forty days. They found it as God had promised, rich, fertile and lush. In fact, on their return trip they cut a cluster of grapes and it was so big they had to hang it from a pole and it took two men to carry it. Now that would be some kind of a grape cluster, even in California!

When the spies returned, there was a big meeting and they made their report. There was a majority report and there was a minority report. According to the "Prater paraphrase," the conversation might have sounded like this:

Ten of the spies were negative. "The land is rich, that is true," they said, "but it's full of giants. They're so big they'd make the Oakland Raiders look like midgets! They are so tall when we looked at them, we felt like grasshoppers. They're too much for us. Forget Canaan, we can get along without milk and honey, anyhow!"

But Joshua and Caleb gave the minority report and Caleb said, "Let us go up at once and possess it for we are well able to conquer them. It's a wonderful country ahead and the Lord loves us. It's a land flowing with milk and honey . . . and don't worry about the giants, the Lord is with us, don't be afraid of them.''

It was that last statement that got my attention, ''The Lord is with us . . . don't be afraid of them'' (Numbers 14:9, TLB). When I read that, the fog began to lift rather rapidly.

The story concludes by stating that the people voted with the majority report and as a punishment they were shut out of the promised land. They wandered about in the wilderness until their lives were over and only Joshua, Caleb and their families were permitted to enter at last.

That story says to me that every person reading these pages lives among hundreds of giants that surround him in his little world. Any one of those giants is capable of clobbering us with the blahs, the troubled heart. Whoever says he knows no giants in his life is either not facing reality or he has just not been paying attention!

We live in a land where there is milk and honey to be had from life. The abundant life has been promised us by the Saviour Himself, but far too many people are shut out of it because they are fearful of the giants. The mere *threat* these giants pose is enough to defeat them.

But Caleb said, ''The Lord is with us . . . don't be afraid of them.'' Well, what are some of the giants we all face? There are, as I said, hundreds of them, but let's concentrate on just two or three blah-bringers and see if we can find the blah-blotter!

THE GIANT WHO LIVES WITH EVERYONE

First there is the giant of *inferior feelings*. He causes a lack of a sense of self-worth, putting a low value on one's self. The psychologists call this an "inferiority complex."

Would you be surprised if I said this giant lives with everyone? "Oh," you say, "I don't believe that. Why I know many people who don't have that problem. They are obviously in charge of their lives. They are self-assured, they've got things going their way, they don't feel inferior to anybody!"

Poppycock! Don't you believe it! The jauntiest, most self-confident, outgoing people you know are as insecure in this matter as most everybody else.

Dr. Paul Tournier hits the nail on the head in his little book, *The Strong and the Weak.* The basic premise in this book is that there really are no "strong people," as such. There are only people who have successfully masked over their inner feelings of inferiority and have learned to cleverly disguise them. At times, claims Tournier, everybody feels inferior. I couldn't agree more.

What a giant blah-bringer this one is! He is perhaps the most formidable barrier standing between us and the abundant life!

And this inferior-feelings giant is a ventriloquist. He can throw his voice and sometimes he throws it right into our minds. We hear his many voices chattering incessantly inside us. Surely you have heard him:

"My nose is crooked. I'm too short. I'm too tall. What if they don't like me? I'm too fat. I could never speak in public, much less pray. Why do other people get all the looks, all the talent, the good figures? I'm dumb. I'm a slow learner. I wonder what they're saying about me? We haven't heard from them in a long time, they must be miffed!"

On and on this kind of nonsensical sewage sloshes through our minds, the harsh, lying, condemning, frightening voice of the giant called feelings of inferiority.

Let's describe the dramatic extremes on both ends of the spectrum of inferiority. At one end are the extremely shy people, the recluses, the hermits, people who shut themselves up in houses and never, never come out in public.

When I was a small boy we lived in a town where there was a recluse who lived with her sister. Neither ever married. The sister would appear in public, buy groceries and do other necessary chores, but this lady never came out. For forty years she lived thus and no one in the town ever laid eyes on her. Of course all kinds of stories spread around. One story claimed she had lived in the city, murdered someone and had fled to our town. Another said she was a witch who came out after dark and lay in wait for children.

Actually, I am sure she was a most insecure person who had lost the battle with the giant who had invaded her life. When she died there were brief services in the local funeral parlor. A good many curious came, but her sister honored her life-style and the coffin was not opened.

Now swing across with me to the other end of the spectrum and take a look at Adolph Hitler. A giant identical to the one within the life of the spinster recluse tormented Hitler, too, but there were different symptoms. Hitler was an illegitimate child, and he grew up with the deep down knowledge that he was rejected, unwanted and unloved.

His giant turned him into a driver. The burning drive

and obsession of his life was to prove he was not just equal to but better than other men. He had a terrible need to prove himself. His desire for self-worth was insatiable. It drove him to be the dictator of Germany and the conqueror of most of Europe, but that was not enough. He wanted the world!

You know the sad ending as well as I. After forty million people perished because of his insane lust for power, he finally lay dead in a German bunker. He supposedly took his own life with a pistol. Actually the giant of inferior feelings had slain him long before.

I used to know a person who was likeable, affable and handsome. Personality and charm oozed from him like toothpaste from a tube. He had talent to spare. He was a driver and a dashing success. He had everything most of the rest of us would love to have.

But he was also constantly boastful, brash, impulsive and a bit overbearing. He dominated his wife and children. He manipulated people, he hungered after position and status. He was a real "go-getter."

In spite of his success, many people did not like him and shunned his company. This seemingly did not bother him as he went on his merry way, breezing along, seemingly getting more than anyone from life.

But one day he sat in my study. I do not know why, but that day he wanted to talk and share his very deepest heart with me. Finally, all the brave self-assurance fell away and the tears stood in his eyes as he said to me, "Did you know that I am an orphan? Yes, my parents didn't want me. They left me in a basket at the doorstep of an orphanage. I never knew who they were."

Afterwards, I went off and wept a bit because I had been so busy being offended by his overbearing nature, I had failed to hear his cries. I had failed to see the giant who dominated his life, standing between him and the land of milk and honey.

If it makes us feel any better, even kings must battle this giant. King Saul had been anointed by God. He stood a head taller than everybody else and he had all the characteristics of an outstanding person. Yet, on the day of his coronation, he ran away from the festivities and they found him hiding among the baggage.

All these, of course, represent people at the extremes, the ultra shy and the ultra pushy. In between is everybody else. Each one of us has his or her own set of symptoms and on occasion our giant emerges to make us feel like grasshoppers!

A bit further on we'll talk about handling this blah-bringer, but for now let me simply repeat for all of us what Caleb said: "The Lord is with us, don't be afraid of them!"

THE GIANT CALLED PRESSURE

Here's another giant who wades the Jordan and plants his feet in our paths to keep us from the promised land. I believe he must be an American giant. His name is "Pressure."

What sheer pressure under which we all live! It used to be you could move out to the country and get away from it all but no more. It just means you have to drive further and faster than anyone else in order to get there on time.

People are wound up inside. A woman told me the other day that she had rushed for twenty-four hours as if she were double-parked!

The pressure giant is raging inside this mechanized, slenderized, transistorized, hypnotized, analyzed, tranquilized, paralyzed, computerized, flip-top-box, hopped-up, freaked-out culture of ours. People don't know where they're going, and if you don't know where you're going, any road you choose will take you there.

No wonder we turn out souls by the gross, stamped in plastic to sell for a quarter. People all about us die prematurely, and you can die prematurely whether you're 18 or 80!

It should come as no surprise then that the leading killer in our country is not cancer or heart disease, but hypertension! Circulatory diseases practically all spring from hypertension. The pressure giant! We have 65% of the wealth of the world but consume 90% of all the tranquilizers and sleeping pills that are manufactured! This says to me that we are the most pressurized people living on this wayside planet.

And it's not just men. I don't know of anyone under more pressure than young mothers with children in school! Just being a chauffeur to three or four is almost too much. Somewhere I found a definition of a mother I like: "one who carries her children physically for nine months and mechanically for the next 16 years!"

In my lifetime, I have watched the emergence of three major social syndromes, two of them have about gone from us but the other flowers in full glory.

When I was a boy the syndrome was *holier-than-thou*. If you were "good" you didn't smoke, drink, or play cards (except Rook). When you hear someone boasting that he doesn't smoke, drink, or any one of a dozen things, this is the same ancient syndrome that affected the Pharisee in the temple who stood up to pray and said, "God, I thank Thee that I am not like other men . . ." (Luke 18:11, RSV).

That's the kind of talk about which Jesus said, "You hypocrite, first take the log out of your own eye, and then you can see clearly to take the speck out of your brother's eye" (Matt. 7:5, RSV).

The second syndrome I watched develop was *guiltier-than-thou*. Everybody got together, formed small groups and discussed how bad and how guilty they were. Then they would sit down, form a circle, close their eyes, reach out and touch one another and that took care of that! (I am not anti-intellectual, I am only describing syndromes I have watched develop!)

The third syndrome I have watched come to life is *busier-than-thou*. It is all the rage now in this society of pressure giants. You don't have status at all if you cannot impress people with how utterly devastating your schedule is; where you've been, where you're going, and what you have to do. If you're going to be in it at all, you simply must outdo the other fellow's calendar! "You think you're busy? You think your calendar is full, well, you ought to see mine!" Busier-than-thou. The giant of pressure puts his big foot on our necks and presses us down and down until something's *got* to give!

Now let me tell you who this giant is. He is a first cousin to the giant of inferior feelings. They belong to the same family tree. Suppose I meet you and start the busier-than-thou routine. I begin to tell you how "bushed" I am because I've been doing this, and I'm going there, and they want me over there next week, and after that . . . .

When I start all of this what I am really saying is,

"Look, if I'm *that* busy, I must be important, I'm in demand, I'm necessary, I'm wanted, I count for something. If I have to work *this* hard for my family, they must need me very badly. Therefore, as a person I must be worth something after all!"

These are the tactics of the pressure giant. From women he demands spotless homes, sparkling silver, compulsive cleaning. From men he extorts daylight to dark driving and pushing and shoving to make it and make it big!

All this ultimately brings on a king-sized blah that may last for days, weeks or months. It may even eventually break up homes and what's worse, it may tear up people!

So these two cousins stand on the opposite shores of our Jordans, keeping us from the abundant life and reducing us to feeling like grasshoppers.

As I promised, we're going to face them head on, but for the moment, let this suffice: "The Lord is with us . . . don't be afraid of them!"

NOTHING TO FEAR BUT . . .

Of the hundreds of giants about, let's zero in on one more. This giant is fear itself. What a giant fear is! Sometimes I think he is the ancestor of them all! I must say the same thing about him I said about inferior feelings. This giant lives in *everybody*.

In one of his essays Emerson said, "Be kind, every person you meet is fighting a battle." We could safely paraphrase that to say, "Be kind, everybody you meet is afraid!"

Most of us, of course, are not afraid constantly or incessantly. There are times when I'm having fellowship with great souls in some grand conference or retreat somewhere and some tremendous soloist stands up and sings, "Because He Lives, I Can Face Tomorrow!" At times like those, I'm not afraid of anything.

In times like those, my giant just sort of stands back and waits. He is in no hurry. He knows the letdown is coming, the darkness will fall, the circumstances will close in. *Then* he can come and plant his sharp dagger in my heart.

This is true because he knows we live in cycles, that we live in flesh and blood bodies and that our moods are changeable as the weather itself. Indeed, our moods *are* subject to the weather, sometimes.

But when he comes he throws his voices into my mind. I begin to feel the sharp point of his dagger as it probes. That tiny pain in my abdomen, was it the very first warning? Or that twinge in my chest, or that little catch in my hip, especially now that it has lingered for three days, are these the beginning of . . . ?

I do believe I have imagined more heart attacks, tumors and what have you than exist in any sanitarium in the country all because of the subtle, evil voice of the lurking giant we call fear.

"The children won't marry right. I'll have a car wreck. I won't make that deal. I can't make the payments. It won't start raining. It won't stop raining. Prices will go up. I'll lose my hair. I'll be paralyzed . . ." Faster than we can feed them computer-like into our minds our giant lets loose a never ending stream of possibilities. What a giant fear is!

We're like an announcer at an Oklahoma football game. The Oklahoma quarterback broke into the open for a sure touchdown, then slipped and fell flat on his face. The announcer, trying to save the situation, said, "Oh, Oh, the Big Red Quarterback just became the victim of self-tackle-ization!"

So it is with these giants. We just allow them to creep in and we tackle ourselves!

HOW TO SLAY YOUR GIANTS

We have analyzed three of the many giants who stand in our pathway. We all are faced with them, every one of us, the giants of inferior feelings, of pressure and of fear. So what are we going to do about these horrendous blah-bringers?

Well, Caleb was right. We are not to be afraid of them. Caleb did not deny the *existence* of the giants, and we shouldn't either.

Caleb did not deny their reality, he simply said, in effect, "They're there, the majority report is correct, but it's nothing to be ashamed of! The Lord is with us, we *know* that, so don't be afraid of them!"

Because the giants are in your life does not mean you are not a "good" Christian. It does not mean you don't love God. Just don't be afraid of them.

There is no one reading these pages who knows better than I that this is all easier said than done. But perhaps if we understand the *origin* of our giants and what God has done about them, we can handle them and the soul-rankling blahs they bring.

We have these giants because *we have been loved imperfectly*! God's word plainly tells us that "perfect love casts out fear'' (I John 4:18, NASB). We were *made* to be loved perfectly but the human beings around us have been doing a far from perfect job. If we had been loved perfectly, these giants would never have invaded our lives. *But no human being, at this point, can love perfectly.*

It matters not how wonderful your parents were, they did not love you perfectly. You may be the greatest parent to your children in your entire city, but you do not love them perfectly. I think we would all admit to this.

Basically *all* personality damage springs from this very cause. We have been loved imperfectly and *everybody* is seeking fulfillment, identity, actualization, whatever the term, it means the same. We all seek to be that for which we were made!

To say it scripturally, '' . . . all have sinned and fall short of the glory of God'' (Romans 3:23, RSV). Nobody has *loved* as he or she was made to love and nobody has *been loved* as he or she was made to be loved!

So we are all in the same boat. The only difference between us is that our *symptoms are different*. For some, their symptom is the bottle. So please *never* look piously down your nose at an alcoholic, for the only difference between the two of you is your symptoms. His happen to be socially unacceptable; yours may be more subtle and less obnoxious than drunkeness.

The symptoms may include compulsive eating, perfectionism, money drive, power thirst, compulsive talking, a domineering personality, shyness, obsessive cleanliness or any one of a veritable host of others. We are all in the same boat, and the giants are after us, because we have loved and been loved imperfectly. All neurosis springs from that!

Just at this point lies the reason we call the gospel of Jesus Christ "Good News." Now follow carefully, Jesus Christ was wonderfully human and he was wonderfully divine. But He had one advantage none of us have. *He was loved perfectly before the world was.* Therefore, when He came, he brought no giants with him.

He had no giant of inferiority. "I and my Father are one," He said.

He had no giant of pressure. On his way to a dying girl he had time to stop and heal a woman who had touched the hem of his garment.

He had no giant of fear. His very birth announcement began with the words, "Fear not . . ."

Jesus Christ was loved perfectly and the Good News is that *He loves us perfectly*. We were made to be loved perfectly and we were not, but since we have met Him, our need has been met! Jesus said, "As the Father has loved me, so have I loved you" (John 15:9, KJV).

And because He knew at that point His mere words could not be enough, there came a day when the earth darkened and trembled in protest as the Lord of Glory hung suspended between heaven and earth on a crude Roman cross. He poured out His blood and His very life for the precise reason that perfect love demanded it, and He hung there until His life was gone.

They lifted Him down from the cross and carried Him down the hill to a new tomb and there they buried Him. But three days later He arose from the dead and the dominion of the giants over the earth exploded into a million pieces. Love forever climbed upon the throne as

Jesus became the Lord and Master of every giant that ever existed, including sin and death!

And from that day until this the open tomb proclaims, "*Now you have been loved perfectly*! Your damage has been repaired! Now you *can* cross over and claim the milk and honey!"

There is no record that Canaan was a land where the giants were wiped out. But the Israelites crossed over and lived in triumph and victory *among them*!

Daniel was safe *among* the lions in the den, not because they were wiped out!

Now what then are we to *do* when the giants, the blah-bringers come upon us? How do we handle giants of inferior feelings, pressure and fear? We are to do what Peter, the hyperthyroidic swordswinger, told us to do. When he was an old, old man, Peter wrote, "Cast all your anxieties on Him . . ." (I Peter 5:7, RSV).

One translation says, "Unload them . . ." I like that picture—just like a dump truck. The giants come . . . put them in it . . . press the button . . . see the dumpbed slowly raise to full angle . . . then pull the lever. That is your God-given privilege through the lovely Christ. Just simply say to Him, "Lord, here's my giant. He's too much for me today. I unload him on you!" Do it, then turn away to the next task.

Will that giant return? The question is not "will?" but "when?" Giants give up very reluctantly, but they *do* give up. That is the growth-promise held out to every Christian.

As we grow and mature and practice this faith, gradually the giants cease coming so often. Finally, if not here, then in heaven they cease altogether. *Then* all the giants will be gone. *Then* we shall know, even as we are known!

Chapter Five

How About the Red and Green Light Blahs?

Most people I know are overworked, overspent, overtaxed, overanxious and overweight! Too many are underpayed, underyielded, underfaithed, and underhopeful, while most everybody is overlooked and underloved!

No wonder we are a blah-stricken people! Yet there is no way in which I am willing to hand over my sword in abject submission and surrender and give a troubled heart lordship over my life! I hope by now you are beginning to feel the same way.

I hope by now you and I may have begun to discover some of the basic things about ourselves which "make us tick.'' If we have begun to understand why we act and react as we do, then we are beginning to get equipped so that God can give us that abundance of daily life when we ask Him!

Surely as yet I do not pretend to ''know myself'' completely, but just as surely most any of us can humbly say that we know more about ourselves today than we did ten years ago. Wouldn't you agree to that?

It must be a terrible thing to be born, live and die without ever having the foggiest notion just *why* we act as we do!

In these pages we are attempting to build a bridge across the river that divides the shores of ignorance and understanding about ourselves. So at this point let me lay down another very long and firm plank that should immeasurably strengthen that bridge.

Everybody, but everybody is attempting to establish patterns of living in which they ''feel safe!''

And why not? It is a great big world, and we are tiny specks put down in a relatively tiny portion of it. About us are vast numbers of things that threaten our very existence, both personally and corporately. We are living in bodies that constantly must battle disease, cold, heat, drought, famine, poverty. We live in a world where wars erupt in almost every generation, and there are such things as earthquakes, pollution, tornadoes, inflation, taxation. The list seems practically endless.

We must learn to survive by coping successfully against all these constant threats, plus one more—the greatest threat of all. We are creatures who are made to be loved. Being loved and accepted are as vital to our survival as food and air. Since *people* are the only visible source of that earthly love and acceptance, the biggest threat to that survival is guess who? Other people!

No wonder each one of us seeks, in his own little world, to establish a pattern of daily living in which we will feel safe.

Sometimes personality damage causes us to establish patterns within the context of that very damage. You can illustrate this by a potted geranium. Transplant it three times and it will usually die. What happens? Any transplanting is a shock to a plant. After the initial shock, in a few days, it will cautiously begin to put out its little feeler roots, seeking food that will sustain life and give it growth.

But what if you rudely shock it again by tearing it from the flowerpot and setting it in another? After a while, a longer while this time, it will again begin to put out little feeler roots that seek acceptance in its new environment.

But then you yank the plant from the second flowerpot and set it down in a third. This time, it will no longer put out the feeler roots. It has had too many bad experiences. The plant concludes that the only safe pattern is to turn its feelers inward. For a few days it feeds from itself and then the inevitable result is, of course, death.

Similarly, here is a young man who puts out "feelers" from himself toward a young woman. After a while, what at first seemed a promising relationship comes to an abrupt end. She finds "someone else."

This damages his sense of self-worth. He is not so quick to repeat this, but eventually he decides to try again with another girl. Once more the same thing happens. It all begins great but ends when she finds "someone else." Repeat this a few times and you have the stuff from which some bachelors are made! The only pattern in which they feel "safe" is with feelers withdrawn!

Whether the patterns are positively or negatively slanted, we all seek to cope with our constantly threatening environment by establishing situations in which we "feel safe."

That is why change is always a threat to us! It threatens the young less than the older, for the young are still darting about here and there trying to find and establish comfortable patterns of their own.

But (to set an arbitrary figure) when we pass thirty we usually have established some patterns in which we feel a degree of comfort and safety. This is the exact basis for nostalgia in the "senior citizen" group. The longings for the "good old days" are brought forth by the always present signs of change in the upcoming generation.

Somewhere I read that the oldest form of human writing known to us is inscribed in a Phonecian tablet which is set into the corner of a temple in Turkey. Roughly translated, it says "Alas, Alas! Things Are Not As They Were!"

Precisely, and what's more, they never will be! God's word very plainly tells us that *He* is the only Force that does not change. Everything else He has built into His creation is by its very nature constantly changing.

Against life's realities we pit our little patterns of living in which we "feel safe." Once we establish them, it is very painful for us to have them threatened with change, but change they must!

THE BLAHS CALLED "STOP-AND-GO"

All of this brings us to the Red and Green Light blahs! The writer of the book Ecclesiastes lived before Christ came. Because of Jesus Christ we are spared from his glum conclusions, but nevertheless this writer caught a vivid glimpse of the nature of stop-and-go living. In the third chapter he writes, "To everything there is a season, and a time to every purpose under the heaven: a time to be born, and a time to die; a time to plant, and a time to pluck up what is planted: a time to kill, and a time to heal; a time to break down, and a time to build up; a time to weep, and a time to laugh; a time to mourn, and a time to dance . . ." (Ecc. 3:1-4, KJV). He goes on for several more verses, but he is simply making the point that in life things are set up so that something will end in order that something else can begin.

And when our "safe" patterns end, the blahs descend—the stop-and-go-blahs! Here are some simple examples right out of our common human experiences of the "ending-beginning" nature of living.

For a mother her child is really an extension of herself come to life in another person. That is why a man can never feel the precise depth that a mother feels for her child. The child is flesh from her flesh.

From the moment of birth on, the mother's entire world rotates about this new life. The limits of that child's life are set so that it is always within sight of its mother, except for rare short intervals. It's waking and sleeping hours are always spent within a few feet of her. It is accessible to holding, "cuddling" or whatever motherly impulse she may feel. Whatever need the mother or child has, it can be met in a few minutes time.

But because we live with the red and green lights, the time comes for the child to start to school. The pattern of mother-child closeness (physically) is broken. Change has come. An era has ended. The blahs descend upon mother, the stop-and-go blahs.

I remember that day in our home. It was only a short distance to the school. Our son had a year's experience in kindergarten. He didn't want his mother to accompany him. So we stood in the doorway and watched as he bravely trudged off down the street, all alone against the great big world.

I remember how proud I felt that he wanted to go alone. I imagine my chest swelled a bit and a smile of satisfaction played about my lips. But then I glanced at Martha and was utterly astounded to see the tears spilling down her face.

Of course, I do not yet know the precise emotion she felt, but I know something now I could not comprehend then. The pattern with her child in which she "felt safe" had been shattered. There was "heart hurt," loneliness, dismay, a bit of panic and many other mixed feelings welling up within her.

The same kinds of feelings rise up within us every time radical change in our life-style is forced upon us. It can happen at graduation time, weddings, going away to college. Anytime our "safe" patterns must change there are the blahs. The stop-and-go blahs come upon us.

And they *must* be dealt with. Otherwise, negative and neurotic symptoms soon appear. Who has not known of the "possessive" mother, or the "domineering" father? Both are motivated by fear for the "safety patterns," for their reluctance and refusal to yield to change.

Any radical change in life-style brings on a blah-crisis. Losing a job, moving from one community to another, saying "goodbye," welcoming a new family member, even changes in our local social habits can bring these crises on. The list is endless, so suffice it to say we should *know* that a life-style change is going to disrupt our "safety patterns." We *are* going to react in one way or another. The advantage we have is that by knowing, we can better *choose* our reactions.

HOW TO COPE WITH CHANGE

It is our trust in and our fellowship with the Lord that makes us victors and not victims. It is He who has loved us perfectly. It is He who gives us the grace and vision to see the brilliant opportunity that lies hidden within our blah-producing circumstance! We are to love God not only with our hearts but with our minds, and this is what opens up to us our options.

Again, I am no "expert" who has arrived. I am simply trying to share what has worked for me. I have found that the way to handle the stop-and-go-blahs is to set up conditions wherein there is something to *hope for*, something to *do* and someone to *love*!

Let's just illustrate them one at a time. Suppose we know that a change in one of our "safety" patterns is coming. We *know* the child is going off to school, Johnny is joining the navy, our husband is being transferred, whatever. We know what this *does* to us and the dangers it brings, so we *anticipate*.

First we seek something to hope for. We commit the

new with its unknown ending earnestly and honestly to God in prayer. The writer of Hebrews said it so well, "Now faith is the assurance of things hoped for, the conviction of things not seen" (Hebrews 11:1, RSV).

"There goes my little boy down the street, God. I've had to cut him loose. I know that as he goes, he is taking something with him he never had before, his first real taste of independence. I commit him to you, God. I have every faith and assurance that you have a plan for his life. I know you love him more than I. I know that when he returns home this afternoon our relationship will be different, but he will still be Yours and *that* will not change!"

Something to hope for. "We're moving to a new job, Lord. A brand new town, a new group of friends, a new church, a new neighborhood, a new set of people with a new set of needs. My safety pattern is shattered. I could be fear-filled, wondering what they will think of me, wondering if I can measure up. But Lord, even though my pattern is gone, You are not. I trust and believe that You will help me to weave a more wonderful pattern than I ever had here. I'm trusting you, Lord, and I have every hope and assurance I need!"

That's walking by faith. And it fits *any* shattered security pattern. It is *the* great determent to the red and green light blahs!

Then we should set up the second condition—something to do. When we know a particular safety-pattern is coming to an end, plan a pleasant counter-offensive. We need something to help soften the blow, something we love to do. For example, the night after Johnny leaves for the Navy, we will go for a dinner date at that super-special place. Or we will take a second honeymoon. We'll buy some new clothes, charcoal a steak, take a boat trip.

We'll anticipate and *plan* a very special something to which we can eagerly look forward at the same time we're facing up to the reality that *this* certain phase of our life is coming to an end. We have committed the situation to God in faith and hope and now, in addition, we're going to plan deliberately a thing or two that always lifts our spirits. That way there will be an offsetting joy for the shock of letting go of a pattern to which we have clung!

For our third condition we'll look for someone to love. Maybe it will be someone new. We'll volunteer for a social service group, Meals-On-Wheels, Youth Sponsors, something to be of service. The opportunities here are without limit. Every community is crying for people who will love and serve other people through existing agencies.

Or maybe it will be someone familiar. We'll plan a trip to surprise the folks, or call an old friend on the telephone. We'll send flowers to an old teacher, or write a former minister. We'll seek someone to love. We'll show them gratitude, or we'll love them in concrete ways such as sending money, or baby-sitting. If we are loving God with our minds there will be no dearth of ideas.

And if your mind goes blank, then *ask Him*. It is difficult to imagine that a God who is described in His own word as being Love itself will not be able to come up with something or someone through whom or to whom you can show forth His love.

I guarantee that doing these things will handle the stop-and-go-blahs and turn them into brilliant opportunities! If we'll just ask, God will give us eyes to see them!

BEWARE OF THE "FP BLAHS"

There are many varieties of blahs other than the stop-and-go kind. Let's just examine a couple and see if we can apply these principles to them as they appear.

Here's a common blah that I call the "FP Blah!" The FP stands for "Fuzzy Priorities." It appears when we get our priorities all mixed up.

Here you are, sailing nicely along in your little safety pattern and everything is just going great! Then suddenly, without any apparent reason, things begin to come unglued. You have one of those days when you should have stayed in bed. I don't have to describe them, you know them. Nothing you do is right. All kinds of negative thoughts take over. Your dream castles turn into rental shacks. You know only one thing for sure. The blahs have arrived.

Most problems have to do with dealing in the garbage of the past. We make mistakes. Something happens suddenly or something builds up and explodes. And there we are, hanging on to our regrets, wallowing in self-pity! It often happens because of fuzzy priorities—getting things out of focus.

I have seen lots of bumper stickers the past few years but the greatest was bright red on a white background: "HAVE YOU HUGGED YOUR KID TODAY?" I imagine that bumper sticker, with the help of the Holy Spirit, has straightened out quite a few fuzzy priorities along the way.

It is so easy to get our priorities all backward.

Somewhere I read the story of a little boy, who, as the family was at supper, suddenly shouted, "PASS THE POTATOES!"

In spite of his tearful protestations, his mother indignantly sent him from the room. He was banished in disgrace from the family circle for such unseemly behavior. Later on in the evening the father disclosed that he had bought a new cassette recorder that day and was secretly recording the family chatter at suppertime to play later. As they played the recording they heard loud laughter, excited chatter. Everyone was talking at once and then they heard a tiny little boyish voice say, "May I please have some potatoes?" A bit later the same voice said, "Please somebody, will you let me have some potatoes?" The chatter continued and then it came, the great shout, "PASS THE POTATOES!"

Nobody was listening. Everyone was interested only in his own opinions. It was a total family case of fuzzy priorities.

Many, many times I have gone into hospital rooms where someone lay stricken with a sudden heart attack, or some other serious and painful ailment. Often I have heard this statement, "One thing I have learned from this . . . and that is what is important and what is not!" On another occasion I have heard a father cry out after his little boy had died, "Oh, if I only had him back again, how different things would be!"

Fuzzy Priorities.

A doctor friend of mine rode fifty miles to a hospital in an ambulance with a man who had suffered a stroke and was unconscious. His wife rode with him and kept crying and saying over and over, "Oh, he can't die, he can't die, what would I do? What would happen to me?"

It often seems we need a crisis to clear up our fuzzy priorities. But why wait until the stroke, or the sudden uprising, or the collapsing of the safety pattern? Why not *anticipate*? It takes only one morning a month for me to look over all my relationships and involvements to see if my priorities are in proper place. Maybe that is what the Lord Jesus meant when He said so often, "He that hath ears let him *hear*, he that hath eyes let him *see*!"

But what if you have waited too long? It slipped up on you. You got your priorities mixed up and it happened. Now what do you do? Once more remember: something to hope for, something to do, someone to love.

It never helps to take spiritual bubble baths in oceans of self-pity. Now is the time for commitment. "Take it to the Lord in prayer" is more than just a familiar line in an old hymn. It is one of the most thrilling realities ever to sink into an anxious mind. He cares, so *take it to Him*. Ask His forgiveness. Thank Him for finally brushing the scales away from your eyes so that you could see your mixed-up sense of values. Then accept *His* forgiveness.

Some people accept God's forgiveness but cannot forgive themselves. Those who cannot forgive themselves have a problem with pride. What they are really saying is, "How *could* a nice person like me have done a thing like that!"

So accept His forgiveness in hope, and then *do* something. If restitution is called for, do it quickly! Apologize, make a phone call, write a letter, whatever it takes, so long as you don't hurt someone else in the process. Whatever is called for, *do it!* If nothing is called for, *don't do anything*. Sometimes doing nothing is the greatest thing you can do! (More about this later.)

Then find someone to love. Perhaps it will be the person who has been the victim of your misplaced priorities. Perhaps it will not be a person, but an institution, such as your church or your company. Have someone over for a cup of coffee. Pay a visit to one of your old shut-in friends. Start a hospital visitation group or take on some nursing homes. Remember what Jesus said about a "cup of cold water (Matt. 10:42, TLB)? This old world is simply riddled with hollowed out places where there is no love. Go and fill some of them!

For the sake of our very own souls the FP Blahs have to be handled quickly. We cannot dawdle about this. Time is too short and precious. It costs too much to put it off. We can die prematurely, and age won't have anything to do with it!

BE READY FOR THE "S-O BLAHS"

No book could ever deal with all the blahs in life. I am laying down just a few planks here . . . across that bridge that leads to better understanding of ourselves. There is another common blah that can happen at any time (and usually does!). Fortunately, it too wilts under the pressure of the threefold cure!

I'm speaking of the Sudden-Obstacle blahs. Here you are, working hard at establishing the pattern in which you are beginning to "feel safe." You have plans made, maybe for a month ahead, maybe for a lifetime. Then it happens. A great obstacle arises out of nowhere. It blocks you completely and sends wave after wave of sickening frustration into your life.

Your picnic is rained out or your golf game is cancelled. You are struck with blindness, some disease comes upon you or an accident cripples you. Small or large, temporary or permanent, obstacles constantly arise to frustrate us.

I watched a caterpillar crawling across our porch like a bundled up little locomotive. Placing my hand in front of him, he stopped, then turned in a different direction. Everywhere he turned I blocked his path, and he had to choose another way. Finally I tired of the game and let him go.

Then I began to think about how the caterpillar had no real choice in dealing with the obstacle that blocked his path. He could only turn blindly in another direction. But you and I are not made like this. We cannot prevent obstacles that block our paths, but *we can choose our reactions!*

After the first wave of creature disappointment passes we can choose whether or not we will feed the disappointment, saturate ourselves in self-pity and enjoy secretly the pity others bestow upon us. Or we can choose to believe that nothing can defeat our God. We can begin to praise Him as we realize He is not defeated by what has happened. If we will let Him, He can turn an obstacle into an even greater joy than if our original plans had been carried out!

How can you lose with a deal like that! We have His word for it, "We know that in everything God works for good with those who love Him . . ." (Romans 8:28, RSV).

It is very plain that in the beginning Jesus wanted to establish His kingdom by love. His teaching and preaching all pointed in this direction, but He soon saw that there was in His path a cruel Roman cross.

He wept in disappointment outside the city of Jerusalem, and then He made his choice. His disciples sought to dissuade Him from going to Jerusalem, but he "steadfastly set His face" and went. He chose His own reaction. He met His cross head-on and turned it into the best thing that could have happened, to Him and for us!

When you can take the worst and turn it into the best, that is an alchemy that comes only from a loving and all-powerful God.

The beautiful White River rises up out of northern Arkansas and flows into Missouri. Then it turns back south and wends its way back down to the Mississippi and on to the sea. For centuries this has been its "safe pattern," but now engineers have thrown up four huge dams, blocking its pathway and forming great impoundments of water.

If I had been the White River I should have felt the surge of anger, frustration and disappointment rise up within me. How dare they do this? How could they do this to me? I should have become very indignant about the whole thing. How could they disrupt a pattern in which I was so safe and secure?

But was that old pattern the best? Before the dams were built the river provided recreation for only a few, and outside of that it was of little use. Now that same river includes the beautiful Beaver, Table Rock, Bull Shoals and Norfolk lakes. Thousands of people are provided with recreation, but more important than that, hundreds of thousands of people are supplied with electrical power for their living needs.

In the same way God can take the idly flowing

currents of our lives and transform them into mighty forces for good because of the obstacles that come upon us.

I do not believe for a moment that God sits on His throne and arbitrarily sends us obstacles such as crippling diseases, blindness, depression and so on. But the universe is so set up that He allows these things to happen. When they do and the blahs smack us—*then* we can turn to Him in faith, apply the three cure-principles mentioned and His mighty victories will eventually astound us as well as those about us!!!

Jesus would not allow Peter, James and John to stay upon the Mount of Transfiguration and just enjoy the heady air of a great emotional religious experience. Wonderful as all that was, He knew that their growth had to take place down in the dust and grime of the valleys. They had to go where the epileptics were, where the clouds of hatred, greed and bigotry hovered and where the bitter acids of power-thirst ran raw in the city streets!

In order to make some perfumes and other fragrant preparations, oils are squeezed from the petals of roses. It is perhaps more than just interesting that those roses must be picked during the blackest hours of the night. I am told that in the European mountains where most of these roses originate, for many years workers have picked them between the hours of 1 and 2 a.m. Why? Scientists have proven that as high as forty percent of the fragrance of such roses disappears during the daylight hours. The point here does not need laboring.

So what has happened to you? Has your life plan been changed suddenly and radically? Has disappointment come swooping in like a vulture to tear at the wounded flesh of your heart? Has sorrow descended? Have those you love let you down? Has some circumstance you could not possibly have foreseen arisen?

I am trying to bear witness to the fact that after the first perfectly natural shock wave passes, *you have a choice*. You can choose your reaction. You can decide if all this talk about God and believing and faith is for real or not. You can choose to be disillusioned . . . a lot of people do. Life was great while things were going your way, but now that *this* had come along . . . well, that's different! Choose that reaction, feed it and nurture it until it becomes full-blown within, and you will eat constantly of the fruits of bitterness, cynicism and despair.

There is, however, another choice. You can choose to risk everything on the belief that this is an impartial universe, that sorrow, calamity and disappointment come upon the good and the evil alike. *But* it is also a moral universe and God will balance the books at last. You can trust that nothing of ultimate and eternal value will ever be lost to anyone who places his or her confidence in the love and power of God to work good from evil, triumph from tragedy and victory from defeat!

Earlier in this chapter we spoke of establishing patterns in which we "feel safe." We made the point that all of us are constantly doing this. Further, we shall be doing it until our dying day for it is our human way of coping with our environment.

But the goal of life for every follower of the lovely Jesus is to grow toward that day when a pattern of safety will be laid over every area of our lives through faith and trust in Him!

The Living Bible begins the little book of II Thessalonians like this, "From: Paul, Silas and Timothy. To: The church of Thessalonica—*kept safe* in God our Father and in the Lord Jesus Christ" (II Thess. 1:1, TLB, italics mine).

This says to me that we will always be laying down everyday meat-and-potatoes patterns of daily living in which we *feel* safe, but we are growing in order to reach the point where our *trust pattern* in the adequacy of our Lord assures us that we *are* safe!

Paul said it another way after his safety pattern in Christ had been firmly laid down, "No, in all these things we are more than conquerors through Him who loved us. For I am sure that neither death, nor life, nor angels, nor principalities, nor things present, nor things to come, nor powers, nor height, nor depth, nor anything else in all creation, will be able to separate us from the love of God in Christ Jesus our Lord" (Romans 8:37-39, RSV).

That's what I call being "kept safe!" Paul didn't say that obstacles wouldn't occur. He simply said we could not be separated from the keeping power of God. Have I arrived at this point in my faith and trust? Are all of my daily-living safety patterns covered completely by this one great pattern that is not destroyed by anything that can happen?

Have I arrived? I wish I could tell you that I have, but alas, not yet. Whom do you know that has? But I can joyfully tell you that I am on my way! I have seen enough of my patterns ended and destroyed that more and more often I can sing that victory hymn with Paul.

I do not know if I will mature enough in this life to say "in *all* these things I am more than a conqueror . . ."

But I do know that *someday* I shall be able to sing it, if not here, then over there!

So may I just say again with you, I am on my way! I am confident, for Paul said something else that strengthens my bridge of conviction beyond telling: "If God be for us, who can be against us" (Rom. 8:31, KJV)?

God *is* for us, that I know. And therefore, the outcome is not in doubt. There is a story about a great steel mill in the east that had a problem. After they melted the iron ore, tiny little flakes fell from it and remained in the oven. Eventually they began to stop up the forge. In order to deal with the problem, the forge would have to be shut off and cooled down before the cleaning could take place, a time consuming and costly process.

So the Manager called in some of the engineers and asked them to find some other way. They decided to increase the temperature of the fire so that the flakes would be consumed. After months of experimentation they came to the manager and said, "We have failed. These flakes are pure carbon, the solidified energy that the iron ore took from the sun itself. No fire we can build will burn up the sun!"

Can't see the connection between those tiny flakes of pure carbon and our faith in Jesus Christ? In *all* our circumstances can we not say that our tiny bits of trust are indestructible gifts from God Himself? If no fire, men can build, can burn up the sun, doesn't it follow that no trouble life can bring can destroy what God has given? Truly, if God is for us, who can be against us?

We *are* more than conquerors!

Chapter Six

Lost and Found Is For Sheep and Want Ads!

Jesus did not say you could stop hurricanes, cyclones, floods and tornadoes. He simply said you could build your house on something that would stand!

Neither does His gospel at any point indicate a Cloud Nine daily existence where there are no blahs or blah days. But running through that gospel like a flashing thread of gold is the assurance that, while we cannot eliminate them, we can be the rulers *over them*!

All through these pages we have used the blahs synonymously with the troubled heart. They are the same. And who escapes the troubled heart?

We know that a troubled heart is not an indication of

faithlessness or even shallow trust. I suppose no one in the Bible is a better figure of faithfulness than Moses. Yet many, many times, as he led the Israelites through the wilderness, the blahs overtook him. Just read the account again and you will be amazed at the frustration, anger, disappointment, bafflement and impatience revealing itself in the person of Moses.

All of God's saints battled the blahs because of their weaknesses. Peter curses and denied his Lord in order to save his own neck. Paul had a guilt complex that kept him constantly sick (could this have been his "thorn in the flesh?"). Sebastian had an illegitimate son and St. Augustine spent over a hundred nights in houses of prostitution. Martin Luther had a problem with constant swearing and John Wesley had a wife who was a shrew. They used to say, "If your wife was like John Wesley's, you'd be a circuit rider too!"

All of God's saints battled the blahs so what kind of a twisted gospel has made you think that if you *really* loved Jesus, you'd be immune from them? This, of course, is not to excuse us in our weakness but only to make us know for sure that we're all in the same boat!

Really, the dangers that can bring spiritual retardation to our growth do not lie so much in the blahs themselves but in their *consequences*! We cannot keep the blahs away. Yes, we can pray, we can "whistle while we work." We can think positively and all that, but sooner or later we are going to slip and they'll come roaring in!

WHY GOD GIVES US MOUNTAINTOPS

So how do we forestall the consequences that the

troubled heart can bring? Well, let me lay down another key plank as a part of the bridge we are building across that river to understanding:

We have to learn to live through the blahs by hanging on to what we saw on the mountaintop! And not only should we trust in what we saw on the mountaintop, but what we *heard*!

Remember Luke's account of the woman who touched the hem of our Lord's garment? Take a moment and read it again in Luke 8:43-48. Jesus was on the way to the bedside of a dying child. In the press of the crowd He "felt power go from Him" and He knew someone with a special need had touched Him. He asked who it was, and this distraught woman confessed that it had been she. Then the Lord Jesus said, "Daughter, your faith has made you well; go in peace" (Luke 8:48, RSV). That was her mountaintop.

Why did Jesus say it? Power had already gone from Him, and she had already been healed, His mission was urgent; He could have gone rushing on, knowing within Himself she had been healed, and certainly she would have known it.

But he wanted her to have a mountaintop to remember. He verbalized it to her because He wanted her to be able later on to put feeling in its place. He knew there would be mornings when she'd burn the toast, her husband would snap at her, the phone would be ringing. The children would be sick, dishes would be piled high in the sink, raining outside . . . well, you know those kind of days! Who *feels* like a radiant child of the King then? And to pretend is the phoniest thing we can ever do!

So Jesus verbalized it and gave her a mountaintop to

remember. He knew how fickle are our feelings. He knew that because we live in bodies of flesh sometimes our moods are affected even by changes in the barometric pressure! Any doctor, psychiatrist or minister will tell you that it is in the grey, dark days of January and February that patient and counselling loads are the heaviest.

Jesus knew the voices would begin in her mind before long. "Did I really touch Him? Or was it all mere emotion? Maybe I'm not really healed. *What if* (remember the "what if's"?) the flow of blood starts again? What if the whole experience was psychological?"

So Jesus gave her His *word*. That was her mountaintop. And when those burnt-toast mornings arrived and the joy dropped out of life, this healed woman could hold on to her mountaintop and it would see her through.

I can hear her rebuking the voices in the midst of her blahs, "I'm *not* trusting my feelings, wonderful as they can be at times. I'm *not* trusting the circumstances that have grown up out of this day, for this day will pass and there will be a brighter tomorrow. I am trusting *His word*. He said it! God said it! And God does not lie or change His mind or go back on His word. His word is not affected by moods or the weather or by circumstances. It stands forever! He said I was healed and that is good enough for me!"

What do you think kept Paul and Silas from falling apart there in that Philippian jail? There they were, locked in the stocks. It was midnight and they began to sing and pray. In my deepest heart I know that as they sat there in the dark foulness of that prison, Paul's mind flashed back again as it had done so many times to that mountaintop back there on the road to Damascus when a blinding light from heaven swept all his hateful, bigoted, sinful nature away in one great inrush of Calvary's love. With the power in his heart from that great life-changing mountaintop he had no trouble whatsoever in dealing with petty blahs like chains, locked doors and scampering rats!

Think through the scriptures, which are jampacked with examples of people who were carried through shattering situations by what they had seen on their mountaintops. Abraham caught a vision of a city, and it kept him going all through his life. Daniel had been on the mountain long before they dragged him off to the den of lions. Nehemiah rebuilt the Temple in spite of everything, because his mountaintop sustained and saw him through.

And even though it is speculation, I am very sure that out yonder in Gethsemane on the darkest night the world has ever known, the tempter must have whispered in Jesus' ear more than once, "Don't do it! They are not worth it!"

At that moment the heart of Jesus was surely troubled. He said it was. But his mind must have gone back to that day when He came upon a great crowd of people who were being baptized by His cousin, John, and He himself had gone down into the water. Then as He came out He heard His Father's voice, "This is my beloved Son, with whom I am well pleased" (Matt. 3:17, RSV).

What a mountaintop when a son hears his father say words such as those! It surely was a mountaintop for

Jesus and it must have stayed with Him through the very doors of death itself!

TIE ON AND DON'T LET GO!

So now the blahs have come upon you. The bubble of life in which you were so safely encased has suddenly burst. Any one of a thousand giants has come upon you and the blahs have struck you down! Well, now we know that mountaintops are not meant to live on, but to tie onto.

So what did you see back there? What did you hear back there on your mountaintop? What grand inner assurance did God give you? Did He not let you know clearly that at *that* point you were traveling the right road? Was He not real in a way that He had never been real before? Did not the insight and understanding flow like a mighty river?

Then hold onto that! Feed from that! This is not to say that we are to live *in* the past, not at all. This is only saying that we are to feed *from* the great moments in our past. That is why God gave them to us, to be used farther down the road.

"But I have had no great mountaintops to remember," you tell me. "I have not been on the road to Damascus. No blinding light experience has ever been mine. I'm just not the emotional type!"

There are surely many, many people who for a variety of reasons have never experienced the deep emotional inrush of God's Spirit in a *feeling* manner. But *everybody* can experience the assurance of God's love and care in a *knowing* manner!

Let's return again to the woman who touched the

hem of the Lord's garment. He healed her. It was physically and emotionally done in an instant, but that was not enough and He knew it. Then He gave her the mountaintop of His word that her faith had made her well.

This is the exact mountaintop that He has given to all people, no matter what their emotional makeup. We all have God's word!

As wonderful as they may be at times, none of us can depend ultimately upon our feelings or lack of feelings. The Bible is God's word. It doesn't change; its very pages declare that the word of the Lord will endure forever. And if *He* said it, then it is true, or else He is not God!

Therefore, the next time the blahs (symptoms of a troubled heart) come upon you, if you have no other, you can let *His word* be your mountaintop. He will see you through by that alone!

How many times have people come to me and said, "Lately, I just feel as if God has left me. I can't get through to Him. It seems He is a million miles away! I feel as if I have lost Him!"

I don't know of any blah more common and universally experienced than this. But it is a classical and *brilliant* opportunity to put our feelings in their place and let the mountaintop of His word see us through. As they say in the Navy, "Now hear this:" "I will never fail you nor forsake you" (Heb. 13:5, RSV). What does this say? This says we have God's word, sealed by the Holy Spirit, that God will never leave us. Therefore, no matter what we *feel*, that doesn't ultimately have a thing to do with it! Friend, if you are God's child through faith in Jesus Christ, you can't get rid of Him. You cannot "lose God." Lost and found is for sheep and want ads; it's not for your relationship with God!

How could there be a mountaintop higher than that?

SOMETIMES IT'S BEST TO WAIT

Now let me lay down another plank in our bridge leading toward understanding. *In the darkness, sometimes we need to wait until the light comes to us!*

So anxious, we are so "pushy." If there was anything Jesus was not, it was that. His life was so completely swallowed up in God, He didn't have to be.

But most of us are too anxious. We think we've got to be plunging ahead. We must be doing something—action, action, action! So, when the blahs baptize us, and no immediate answer or relief comes, we are inclined to take off in all directions.

And since there is no light, only darkness, we stumble, we bumble, we fall. We mess things up in general. Sometimes we need to wait for the light, realizing that when God puts us on "hold" there is always a reason!

Here was Moses on the banks of the Red Sea with the bloodthirsty Egyptian army behind him and the raging tempest ahead. If Moses had been an American he would have shouted "Let's disperse! Everybody for himself! Form a committee! Hold a conference! Let's devise a crash plan! We need a task force! Somebody *do* something!''

But instead, Moses remembered his mountain. On it he had seen the face of God, so instead he said, ''Stand still and see the salvation of God!'' (Ex. 14:13, KJV) The two key words are ''*Stand still.*''

There is a time for action and there is a time for standing still. A time for waiting, waiting for the light to come.

But is there anything we can do while we wait? Yes. We can look for signs. We are God's people and God's people have always asked Him for signs, to know if something is true or untrue. We have always tried to force God to prove Himself. ''Lord, move that picture on the wall, move that star over here, make this room shake, give me a big charge of electricity. Give me a sign, Lord, and then I'll know for sure what to do!''

Wesley and his preachers used to drop the Bible and let it fall open. Then they would shut their eyes and point to a verse for direction. The only problem was that most of the time the verse didn't suit their purposes, so they'd drop it again and again until they got a verse that would do!

God *does* send us signs, constantly and incessantly. The trouble is we are too immature to see them. We have been conditioned to trust in things we can perceive only with our five senses, and so those are the kinds of signs we keep waiting for God to unleash.

But spiritual maturity comes as we see that when we are asked to stand still, or when we are allowed to wait, *that in itself* is a sign. God's silence is a sign. Unanswered prayer is a sign. Paradoxically, unanswered prayer is many times an answer.

DEALING WITH THE "GOD IS SILENT" BLAHS

What a case of the blahs Noah must have had. There he was, with his family, no land in sight, floating around on an endless ocean in the contraption he had thrown up on the backside of his farm. It must have been beastly (if you'll pardon the expression) hot, and with all those animals aboard . . . well!

The rains were over, the waters were calm and they were just drifting, drifting, drifting. Noah had trusted that he had heard God's voice. He had trusted that he had done what God asked. He had trusted that he was where he was because he had done the will of God.

But he had not heard anything further, and they drifted around in the vast and complete silence of the endless waters for two hundred and fifty-seven days! Think of that!

Talk about the blahs, talk about despair, doubt, anxiety. What thoughts would I have had in such a situation? "Maybe God has forgotten us. What have we done wrong? What is God like anyhow that He should allow such things as this to happen?"

I wonder if Noah got the "what if" blahs? "What if that really wasn't God I heard? Suppose I've just gone too far with this religion thing? What if the waters never go down? What if we just drift around out here, run out of food and die? What if all those people who made fun of us were right?"

Two hundred and fifty-seven days! I would have been complaining and a bit disgusted with God if I hadn't heard from Him in a week or so, but try to imagine two hundred and fifty-seven days! Mercy!

Yet, right in the midst of this darkness, there was a

glorious sign—the sign of silence. Silence can be a blessed and glorious sign? Yes it can, if we are His, if we are praying, if we are asking without ceasing!

Silence can mean that we are finally mature enough for God to trust us with no answer for a while. If you are reading this with a troubled heart, I want to ask, has God put that kind of trust in you, the kind that trusts you with His silence? Or are you still weeping and pounding on His door, frantically pleading for a visible answer? Are you despairing before Him because you have had no visible results?

Don't you know that God is going to answer your prayer, but that other people are involved also? Sometimes He has to put you on "hold" while He works with them to try and bring them around to the point He can say "yes" to both of you! Can you not see that He has said inwardly, "Ah, this one can be trusted with the darkness, with My silence, this one can be trusted to 'wait upon the Lord'."

Sometimes, if you pound hard enough on His door and scream loud enough He may sigh and say, "Well, all right . . . here's your visible sign." But you may have just cheated yourself out of the larger and greater blessing He wanted to bestow if you had trusted His silence enough to stand still and wait!

He was going to reveal a deeper thing of the Spirit than you had ever comprehended before, but you panicked and frustrated His loving intention. He was going to work a greater miracle than that for which you had asked, but you could not wait until He finished His work with the other persons involved.

He wanted to stretch your horizons and give you a bigger picture of the love and care He had for you, but instead, through your free choice and His own self-limitation, you shot down His intention because you got pushy.

So if God has blessed you by giving you His silence, the longer it continues the more you should lift up your praise. Praise Him for considering you mature enough to accept the silence. Praise Him because His purposes are going to be worked to fruition through it.

Then one day, in the darkness, you can pray and when there is nothing but silence for an answer, you can say inwardly in joy, "He trusts me, God trusts me." And you can wait in the darkness until the light comes to you!

The darker the night and the louder the silence, the more we give thanks! Many years ago I read the story of a man who was shipwrecked on an island. He was Robinson Crusoe in real life. He survived only by his own ingenuity and perseverance. He lived the hard pioneer life of the wilderness for many months.

Being a deeply religious man, he prayed constantly for rescue. He stormed heaven's gates, day after day. But the months passed, and he began to grow a bit angry and resentful that God should treat him so shabbily.

One day his crude hut, holding all his meager possessions, was struck by lightning during a rain squall and everything went up in smoke. This was the last straw, and he cursed and beat upon the ground in anger and disappointment.

But that very day a ship came and he was rescued. The first words the captain said were, "We saw your smoke signal!" God trusted him with silence until the ship could be in the right position to see the fires of seeming disaster. Only then could God turn his calamity into blessing!

Sometimes, when the blahs come, God trusts us with his silence. That is when we need to rejoice, to stand still and wait until the light comes to us!

HOW TO SPOT "SIGNS OF SMALL AFFIRMATION"

Let's go back to old Noah again for a moment and see if we can gain something else from his experience. God not only sent Noah the sign of silence, of unanswered prayer. When God finally was ready, the sign He sent was a *small affirmation*. If we are mature enough to accept God's silences in faith that He is at work in all things for ultimate good, then we surely need to be mature enough to believe the signs of small affirmations.

On the two hundred and fifty-seventh day Noah finally ran out of patience and sent out a raven and a dove. The raven was "missing in action" and never returned. When the dove returned it was completely exhausted.

So they drifted around for seven more long, seemingly interminable days. That week must have seemed longer than all the rest combined for they had tried something and failed. At this point Noah could well have said, "That does it! God really has deserted us. I've had it with trust. I've had it with prayer. It's all self-delusion anyhow!"

But instead, after seven days he sent the dove out again. And this time the miracle happened. This time the answer came. This time God said, "Now it is time for me to unloose the blessing of understanding!"

So the dove returned to the ark and in her bill she carried a single, olive leaf about the size of a dime, but it was *green*!

That surely must have spoken volumes to Noah. The waters had subsided, the green meant God had not given up on the earth. He was still breathing Himself into it. There would be a second chance and a new beginning. This tiny leaf must surely have spoken all the hope and assurance that mankind could ever have. God had been at work all the time. God had been preparing the way for a new epoch, to be consummated at Calvary and the open tomb in ways that Noah could never really imagine!

But the leaf was so tiny, so very pitifully small, in the midst of all that vast ocean. Noah could have said, "It was a fluke . . . somehow the leaf drifted and stayed green all those days." His mind could have bought a whole set of rational lies, but instead Noah believed in the sign of a small affirmation. I dare say there was quite a celebration aboard that creaky old box that night!

Perhaps the blahs have you and you keep waiting for a great and mighty affirmation. Don't you know by now that, even after the long silence, the affirmation that finally comes will probably be tiny? If God only sent His mighty affirmations, faith would wither. Instead of growing minds that will someday be like Christ's, we would curl up and die spiritually.

Once in a while, to some little sinking disciple who has run out of gas, God grants a mighty affirmation. Most generally, however, His sign of affirmation always has been and probably always will be the size of an olive leaf.

If we believe the Bible we ought to know that by now.

To a little shepherd boy named David, put up against the giant Goliath, He gave what? A twenty millimeter cannon? A sidewinder missile? No, just five tiny little rounded stones. To Elijah, confronting the priests of Baal, he gave only a tiny cloud, the size of a man's hand. To Moses standing on the banks of chaos with the enemy close behind He gave what? A division of tanks? A hundred thousand chariots? No, just a crooked stick.

To Israel, which was looking for the mighty affirmation of a messiah coming on clouds of glory accompanied by the hosts of heaven, what did He give? Only a tiny wriggling baby in a cow's stable behind a crowded inn in a sleepy little town nobody ever heard of!

HAVE YOU SEEN ANY OLIVE LEAVES LATELY?

A great crisis, a great cry, a great despairing, and God offers us a tiny green olive leaf. When will we ever learn that this is almost always His way?

So God has trusted you with a long, almost unbearable silence and now I must ask, can you have trust sufficiently to praise? Can you have perception enough to look for olive leaves and can you recognize one when it comes?

You might well ask me the same thing. Have I seen any olive leaves lately?

Well, yes, as a matter of fact, I have! I was being trusted with a silence. Not for two hundred and fifty-seven days, but still a silence. So after a while I sent out my dove. And a few days ago it brought me an olive leaf.

We were to have our annual organizational meeting

when a card from one of our dear members arrived. With her permission I want to share it with you:

"'Dearest Arnold and Martha,

To let you know I won't be able to attend the annual meeting, much to my regret. But I'll be in Houston with this thing called cancer. Sure could use your prayers.

But praise the Lord I've found there is a work for Him even in the cancer world. *What a blessing He has bestowed on me!* (Italics mine)

Sincerely,
Norma''

It was Black Melanoma cancer, but she could still count it a blessing that she had found a ministry to others in the midst of her own suffering!

When I read that, my dove flew right into the midst of my drifting ark. In her beak there was a single green olive leaf and my heart leaped within. And that on which I have risked everything—my life, my health, my family, everything—flared up into reality once more in a conflagration of affirmation!

Affirmation that good is greater than evil. The spirit is more than the flesh! Goodness is mightier than hate! Love is triumphant over death! Oh, how we celebrated God's goodness in giving us our olive leaf that day.

He is the God of the tiny, the small, and the unlikely. So when I look out across this war-weary, evil-invested planet, scarred with hate-bombs and dotted with graves, this thought comes pounding into my mind with thrilling awareness. It brands its truth into my consciousness with all the concentrated neon of heaven's illumination.

There are thousands of mountains in the world, rising to their mighty heights—the Rockies, the Himalayas, the Pyrenees, the Andes. But God chose one tiny little hill far away on which to plant His Old Rugged Cross. And down that hill just a ways, there is a tomb that is empty! *That* is humanity's olive leaf in the midnight of despair!

Has God trusted you with His silence? Stand still and wait for the light to come. When it does, your olive leaf will come with it.

And while in the darkness it is such a wonderful thing for us to remember that our precious symbol for the Holy Spirit is not an ark or an ocean, or a rain cloud.

It is a dove!

Chapter Seven

Things Are Not as Good as You Thought, They're Better!

Trying to alleviate a spiritual hangover with a pill is like trying to catch a bus by standing still. It cannot be done.

This is not to make light of medicines; it is only to state that there are no physical cures for spiritual ailments.

You woke up this morning and there they were . . . the blahs . . . the troubled heart. You went through all the known causes of previous blahs, the giants, the FPs, the Stop-and-Go kind. You went through them all and none seemed fit. There is simply no reason at all for you to be the victim of the blahs today. It was not a burnt-toast morning. The sun is shining. Life has been smooth for a few days and no major crisis looms. As far as you know, you are physically ok. But there's no use denying it. The blahs are there.

This could be a spiritual hangover. This could be the residue of some broken relationship, or some alienation that you have pushed down into your sub-conscious mind. Now, after some time, maybe a long time, it has festered and the fetid mist is beginning to rise up into your conscious mind where it must be dealt with.

THOSE MYSTERIOUS RELATIONAL BLAHS

After all these years of following Him I have come to one conclusion: the Christian faith is *relational*! We may pride ourselves on our biblical knowledge, our correct theology, our satisfying experiences. But if what we believe hasn't changed us at the point where our lives touch the lives of others, then it is all as phony as a three dollar bill!

In particular it has to work with those you love the very most *and* with those who simply cannot stand you! There is no argument about this if we read the New Testament honestly.

I am not talking about someone's response to you. I am talking about your response to them, the monkey that is on your back. Who is it that makes it harder for you to be a Christian? A friend of mine said that our true love for God can be measured by the extent of love we have for our worst enemy. *That* is something to chew on for a while!

Unresolved alienations are poison to the spirit. Ultimately they make us sick, if not in our bodies, then in our hearts. If we continue to stew in our own juice, it eventually turns to bile.

Talk about people trapped in the ghettos of our great cities! There are thousands of spiritually ghettoized Christians who are trapped by tiny little stagnant pools of resentment, ill will, unresolved alienations and festering grudges.

If I ask, "What is the one thing in my life that keeps me from being my best?" I almost always discover way down there somewhere a clouded relationship. And that clouded relationship is the cause of my "mysterious blahs."

If these blahs are not dealt with, they always eventually externalize themselves in some kind of physical manifestation. The phrase "she makes me sick" can become literally true.

We know that medically some forms of migraine headaches are mechanisms of retreat, which the body provides for us so we won't have to face certain realities.

It can be verified medically that some forms of allergies, rashes, ulcers, arthritis, and many other human physical afflictions rise straight up out of damaged relationships. They are all inner spiritual problems externalizing themselves physically.

But before these tangible afflictions appear they are almost always preceded by periods of the troubled heart. Many times these vague, uneasy feelings are impossible to trace unless we honestly look down into the deep mirror of our relationships.

A woman I knew had a violent argument with her sister over one of their mother's antique pitchers. After a while they "patched it up" on the surface. But several years later, this woman, sickly, bedfast, with a window ledge full of pill bottles, told me when I visited her that she "never had quite forgiven her for it!"

This is not to say that every physical sickness springs from alienations. Nor is it to say we are to spend all our time in introspection for too much of this is unhealthy. If God had meant us to look inward all the time, He might have turned our eyes around. But it is to say that when the "vague" or the "no reason" blahs arise, here is one area that must be carefully examined and scoured out.

HOW TO BE RID OF THE "NO REASON" BLAHS

And if you discover such a simmering pot of poison, what should you do? I do not think anyone who has read this far in this book needs to be told the answer to that! But then pride takes over and the voices begin to protest in our ears:

"But I was right!"

"Why should I go to him, I'll meet him halfway!"

"Why should I apologize for something that was not my fault?"

"They started it, not I!"

"Why should I ask forgiveness for something I didn't do?"

"I'm ready when she is!"

And on and on. The voices seem to have a rational lie to fit every situation. So, here again, let's turn to the Word for our answer.

> "So if you are offering your gift at the altar, and there remember that your brother has something against you, leave your gift there before the altar and go; first be reconciled to your brother, and then come and offer your gift" (Matthew 5:23-24, RSV).

Read carefully. The above does not deal with *who* was at fault. It does not deal with who wronged whom or how it all came about. It contains no instructions whatsoever that apply to the other party, only you. "*If you . . . remember that your brother has something against you . . .*"

Jesus is talking about the *relationship*. He is telling us we need to go and ask forgiveness for *allowing the strained relationship to continue.* We were wrong in allowing it to fester and turn to acid.

We need to say, "No matter who was to blame, I was wrong in making no effort. Please forgive me and let's go on from here!" Then we can come back to our altar with a clean heart. And happily, more often than not, the relationship is healed.

After we have done what we know we must do (and *do it we must*), it is a grand spiritual exercise to arise each morning, stand at the window, look out on God's world and affirm aloud, "*There is not one person on earth against whom I hold the slightest malice or ill will! There is not one damaged relationship I have not tried to make right!*"

When we can say this, we have eliminated one of the mightiest causes for the "no reason" blahs. Not only that, we have taken a great leap in growing away from spiritual dwarfism!

WHY THE BLAHS ARE BRILLIANT OPPORTUNITIES

Now I've come to the very heart of everything we have been trying to say in these pages. The blahs are not just "bad days" that are naturally bound to drop into our lives occasionally with a dull thud.

To those who are blind and who do not read God into daily living, the blahs are things that should be handled with remedies that deal with headaches, upset stomach and acid indigestion. But to those who have been given spiritual eyes with which to see, the blahs are brilliant opportunities! They are red warning lights on the dashboard of life that indicate something needs our *immediate* attention.

The blahs are really a language by which the Holy Spirit is trying to tell us that we are out of kilter in our relationship with God. With the exception of the blahs of fresh grief, they are always saying to us, "Something in your relationship with your heavenly Father needs your immediate attention. Just as unbridled joy means things are right with Him so the blahs mean something is out of kilter!"

Remember once more that we are not dealing with God's *acceptance* of us. That was settled at Calvary. What we are dealing with is our struggle for Christlikeness *in the now*.

So *the language of the negative is equally as meaningful as the language of the positive*. We need not have the language of joy interpreted to us, because we can read that loud and clear. But the language of the negative is not so easy to read and before we can make it out, we must first become convinced that it *can be read!*

Am I bored? Boredom is a negative experience. Boredom should turn our warning indicator light on. What does my boredom have to say about my relationship with God? What needs my immediate attention? What have I allowed to creep in that should not be there? Is self-concern becoming the dominant drive in my life? When self-concern becomes dominant it is a first cousin to self-pity, and self-pity is the acolyte who burns incense before the altar on which the ego sits!

Am I afraid? What does that blah have to say to me about my relationship with a God who wrote into the Bible the words "fear not" exactly three hundred and sixty-five times?

Am I overly tense and anxious? What does that say of my relationship with Him who promised that if He fed the birds and clothed the lilies, He would surely see to my needs?

Is guilt constantly nipping at me? What does it mean if, after asking His forgiveness, I cannot forgive myself?

Is *He* not trying to say something to me through my negative experiences? If He is, then each one of them is a brilliant opportunity, an opportunity to turn my immediate attention to correcting the conditions out of which they arose. The blahs become vehicles that God uses, with our consent, to firm up sagging spiritual muscles, and to give us growth and help.

So just as God was not defeated by the cross, but turned it into the best thing that ever happened to us, He is still using the negatives as instruments through which He can work ultimate positive good!

We can rejoice then in all things, even the blahs, *not* because they happen, but because God is not defeated by them. More than that, He will indeed work in us—growth and beauty. He will transform our blahs into purposeful vehicles through which He can work His will. And to *allow* Him to do this with our free will is what it means to live by faith! "We know that in everything God works for good with those who love Him . . ." (Romans 8:28, RSV).

This, then, is why the troubled heart is always a brilliant opportunity!

THE BIGGEST BLAH OF ALL

As we have said, we could not possibly deal with all the blah-bringers, only those that are most common. So I have left the greatest and most universal bringer-of-the-troubled heart until last, the blah of sorrow.

It was about this one that Jesus spoke when He said, "Let not your hearts be troubled." It is universal and because of the X factor of death written into the nature of the universe, no one escapes it.

The title of this book came about because of a conversation I had with a very grand lady who lives in the mid-south in a small town. When she told me the name of her community, she said, "It's a small town with nine hundred souls living in it. Seventy-five of them are widows and seventy-four of them have the blahs!"

She said it in a very light-hearted manner, yet I thought I heard pathos in that statement. She never knew it, but it touched me to the very depths of my being. I thought about it for days, how such a situation is multiplied by hundreds of millions of people across this planet.

There is not a block in your city which has not been touched by the blah of sorrow. It affects people you meet downtown, at the mall, in the parking lots. It eats at those you pass on the freeways and in airports. Everywhere there is etched on the hearts of most the scars of sorrow. Some are bearing still fresh wounds. They are bleeding very near the surface as they try to cope with it.

It is universal. You somehow thought you might escape, but now it has come upon you. You noted it all about you. You read of it in the papers. Newscasts bombarded you with it. Radios blared it forth, songs proclaimed it, magazines headlined it . . . but somehow your mind never quite accepted the fact that it could happen to you.

But it did, so now what? First of all you must face the reality that just as there is day and night, sleeping and waking, hot and cold, so there is joy and pain in the world. We are stretched between life's opposites like a violin string. Too tight and we break. Too loose and we fail. But held properly in the Master's hands and tuned by Him, there is the brilliant opportunity to make lovely music.

A farmer in Tennessee told me one autumn day, "The soybeans are ripe, but the cockleburs are still green. We must wait until they ripen too, because the combines won't function properly unless both are ready."

So the reality is that the good and the bad, the joyful and the painful must be harvested together. The cockleburs are with us, and whoever turns away from this reality lives in delusion and fantasy. His harvest will be bitterness and despair.

Jesus recognized His hour for suffering and sorrow when it came and He said so: "The hour has come for the Son of Man to be glorified" (John 12:23, NASB).

Christ was glorified and used for God's purposes and we are helped and strengthened, not because God keeps us from our hour, but because He loves us enough to allow us to experience it.

"But how can there be any brilliant opportunity in my sorrow? What I loved most on earth is gone. Every safe pattern I had has been fractured. Nothing will ever again be as it was." That's how we might reason if we face sorrow without accepting reality. But once the first shock waves of sorrow have passed, it is far better to accept reality and ask, "What can God teach me in this? What is my opportunity now?"

Well, first it should be made clear. Sorrow does not automatically grow character any more than sugar in a bowl sweetens. It must be applied, and used.

One thing sorrow can do is blast a lot of shallowness out of our lives. If we seize the opportunity it offers, we can find out who we are!

You cannot find out who you really are in the heady, ego-lifting, glamorous hours up on the mountaintop. You cannot find out who you really are in the pleasantly steady days of the routine.

It is only down in the dark diamond mines of suffering and sorrow that you can find your true identity. You either perish down there, or rise to the surface again, bearing the gems of assurance, trust and serenity in one hand and the scars of battle in the other.

Jesus knew who He was. And it is no accident that the ancient prophet said of Him, ". . . a man of sorrows, and acquainted with grief . . ." (Isaiah 53:3, KJV).

Sorrow *is* our lot. We can curse God and rage rebelliously against reality, or we can accept the fact that this is the way things *are*. Later on He will allow us to ask Him why. Surely in heaven He has interview time set aside for that purpose!

If you haven't "been there" you can't know what it's like. Love as you might, you can't give very much help. But whoever loves God and has brought the gems forth from the darkness can become the foundation of strength on which he can reconfirm the faith of others.

So when you have overcome, be sure you try to pass on your strength to someone else. If you don't, your experience has been wasted.

Of course, while your own storm is raging it's not the time to look for ways to help others. That is only the time for facing your boat into the gale. If you are in a storm of sorrow just now, there is a tender little story I once heard that may help.

When one visits Carlsbad Cavern in New Mexico, a guide takes the party through those vast depths and at one level, hundreds of feet beneath the surface, the party is stopped at a landing. The guide says, "You are probably for the first time in your life going to experience total darkness!"

Then all lights are turned off. As the unspeakable blackness envelops the group, a hush falls over them instantly, for total darkness is indeed an awesome thing.

On one such occasion, the group had fallen silent and then a little girl began to whimper and cry. But her father's voice was heard saying, "*Don't cry, darling, there's somebody here who knows how to turn on the lights!*"

Even in your deepest sorrow somebody will begin one

day to turn on the lights for you. And if you will allow Him to do so, He can begin to show you the opportunities that lie brilliantly disguised in all of this.

Here is a suggestion. When the later-on-after-the-storm-sorrow blahs come upon you, deal with them roughly! There are some moods that are for praying about and some are for stomping on! This kind respond when you put your toe into them. Don't take the time to pray about it, just boot them and say, "Come with me, Lord." Then get going! BLAST OFF!

The deepest law written into the tapestry of creation is stated in the Bible several different ways. Here are a couple of them, "Whoever seeks to gain his life will lose it, but whoever loses his life will preserve it" (Luke 17:33, RSV). ". . . unless a grain of wheat falls into the earth and dies, it remains alone; but if it dies, it bears much fruit" (John 12:24, RSV).

I would like to take you with me to Kansas, a few miles from our Missouri home, and show you the vast, waving amber oceans of ripened wheat. We would climb a little knoll and look out across the great prairie and I would say, "You see all of that grain? Enough to make bread for thousands? Well, it's difficult to believe, but it's true. This entire great field was once a cemetery for wheat seeds!"

Whoever keeps, loses. Whoever gives away, wins. Whoever keeps, dies. Whoever gives, lives. That is why I said that in order to gain the riches God has to give us from these greatest blahs, we have to turn our eyes away from ourselves and blast off! Not to consciously receive but to consciously give.

The story is told of a young man back in the dark depression days of the thirties who had a very menial job. Food for his family became very precious. Often all they would have was potatoes. When that happened, he insisted that his wife and children eat the potatoes, the "best" part, while he ate the peelings. Of course forty years ago we did not know as much about the science of nutrition as we do today. We know now that the actual content of vitamins and carbohydrates is greater in the skin of the potato than it is within. As he reached out to give to his family, the young man unknowingly received the greater blessing for himself!

So blast off! A pastor friend of mine told of a lady who, for two long years, made a daily pilgrimage to the cemetery where she had buried her husband. Rain or shine, cloudy or fair, she went. He tried to comfort her in every way possible but to no avail. She seemed intent, after the initial storm of sorrow had passed, on remaining in a bubble of what turned from normal grief into self-pity.

One day as he drove past the cemetery he saw the familiar figure, standing by the grave. He wheeled his car into the cemetery, got out of it and walked over to her. He looked at her for a long moment, and then said rather loudly and firmly, "He is not here! For He has risen just as He said!" (Matthew 28:6, NASB). Then the pastor wheeled and left. It was the shock of reality she needed. She turned outward and from that day began to grow and serve and become.

What brilliant opportunities await us! Your world and mine is so full of needy people. There are not just welfare cases, but also affluent people who are hurting. There are housewives who feel trapped, businessmen who need a true friend, desperate couples who could use a kind act. And every block in America has at least one aged person who's life is shot through with loneliness.

They tell me that *"hock a chainek"* in Yiddish means "beating a pan." Somewhere I heard someone tell that in the slums of some of the huge cities in Europe, if a Jewish woman has problems she cannot bear alone and needs help, she wanders through the streets beating on her pan. Other Jewish women, hearing the noise, will open their doors and invite her into their homes for coffee and talk.

When I heard that story I wondered, "Do some beat on their pans and gain no response?" I am certain that all about us there are desperate, lonely, needy persons at all levels, wandering daily through the streets of their lives, beating on their pans and many are never, never heard!

Get on your way! Blast off! Stomp that blah and go! Today! Now!

I do not know what your particular cup of tea will be. That depends upon the kind of a personality God has given you. I do know that He has a cup of tea for every different kind of personality He ever made!

If you cannot talk, maybe you can be a good listener. How the world needs listeners. All about us are people frantically, though perhaps not consciously, seeking someone to listen to them. Most of us are too busy thinking of what we're going to *say* when our friend pauses. And we never hear the pans banging beneath the surface chatter.

Hundreds of times, people have come to my office across the years to counsel, pray and talk out their problems. I know in my heart the best thing I have been able to do for them, for the most part, is just to listen and care.

So whatever your cup of tea, start drinking it! Get going! Blast off! Whatever will help you spend yourself for the sake of others, do it. Stop crying for yourself and start crying for your brother.

Besides, things are not as good as you think, they're better! Christian people believe that there's more than just this life. The song writer said it well for all of us: "*I'm possessed of a hope that is steadfast and sure . . .*"

There are some advantages to passing fifty. Chief among them is there are some things you stop doubting. There are some things about which the stabbing fingers of doubt quit tormenting your mind. You have finally become totally convinced.

One of these for me is this: *life lasts!* On the other side of death there's more. For me, "If a man dies, shall he live again?" is a closed question. Let the young debate that, I'm convinced. I have enough evidence to satisfy myself by now . . . *life lasts!*

But when you stop to think of it, that's a weird thing to say. No one has ever come back. No one has ever been to the land that is fairer than day and returned with two hundred colored slides, ten rolls of Super 8 film and a drop-of-the-hat running commentary to go with it.

The truth of the matter is we cannot prove it, at least not with litmus paper and a slide rule. It is all a matter of faith how you want to bet your cards.

Life lasts, and I'll be the first to say that it's a weird thing to say on a planet that is dotted with cemeteries and in a country where practically every good sized town has at least two funeral parlors in hot competition.

It's weird but if we have been paying attention we ought to know that God is and always has been a God of the weird and the off-beat. I dare you to tell me if you ever heard of a more weird and off-beat idea than this: that God Himself should be born of a virgin, a backwoods girl from a sleepy little town nobody ever heard of, and in a ramshackle barn at that!

If you think that is weird, what about this? The great God almighty, Who held in His hands the flaming mass and pounded out the creation on the anvil of His divine will is the *same* God Who chose to hang limply upon a crude, Roman cross of unspeakable pain and death!

But there's more. As if all that were not weird and far-out enough, what could possibly be more off-beat than what happened next? When they lifted Him down from that cross He was dead. There could be no doubt about that. There was cyanosis of the lips, a slight stiffening of the joints, the eyes were shut. They jammed a spear into His side and water and blood ran out.

What could possibly be wilder or more absurd than the idea that *this* man who was so *totally dead* should live again? What is more improbable than that sometime within the next three days in that silent tomb there should be a strange stirring, that the grave clothes should be neatly laid aside and that the mighty stone, stamped with the emperor's own seal, should be shoved aside like a pebble? And what is more utterly mad than the statement that because *He* lives, we too shall live!

But the most insane, idiotic thing of all is the hymn that rose up out of impossible circumstances, which we sing every step of the way to the graveyard: "Death is swallowed up in victory. O death, where is thy sting? O grave, where is thy victory" (I Cor. 15:54, 55, KJV)?

Life lasts! Then the voices come and say, "Yes, but does this mighty affirmation work in real, Monday morning situations?" That is precisely where it works the best and as a matter of fact that is the only place it *can* work!

One winter Martha and I sat in a hospital waiting room with another couple, a young minister and his wife, two of our dearest friends. Their little six-and-a-half year old son was seriously ill and we were awaiting the verdict.

The doctor came in and told us as kindly as possible that the child had a brain tumor and that his chances for survival were nil.

Then, with what seemed like the dammed-up frustration all doctors must feel who daily must deal with such things, he said, "It's so sad, and I don't know why it always seems to strike the most beautiful, intelligent and promising children!" Then he left.

The nurse led us to a private room and, of course, after that the tears just flowed as everything in us broke up at the news. After a while we had a prayer together. When we finished, this young father looked up at me out of eyes that had suddenly been set free from the pain and the chaos of the world and said, "Why Arnold, that doctor was wrong. Jeffery is not going to die in a few months . . . Jeffery is not going to die . . . *ever!* Jeffery is going to live *forever!*"

When you can lay your faith up against a diagnosis like that and ten minutes later turn away in total victory, I say that's *some* kind of victory! That's the kind of victory on which you can risk eternity!

Jeffery was a most unusual kind of little boy. He turned his life and care over to Christ when he was only six years old and the next day he said to his mother with almost what might be called a premonition, "Now I'm ready to go be with the Lord!"

Before he died Martha and I went down to visit Jeffery and his family. I walked into his little bedroom and stopped short. My heart leaped within me at what I saw.

There was a poster taped on the wall. Jeffery had hung it there. There were three crosses silhouetted against a dark, angry skyline and across the bottom of the poster, printed in bold letters, were these words: "*The body will die . . . but the soul lives on!*"

The body will die, but the soul lives on. What certainty! Six and one-half years old and Jeffery knew that he knew for certain—life lasts!

When I read that poster the Spirit of God came upon me. The Lamb of God who takes away the sin of the world suddenly showered my soul with a firestorm of little spotted spasms of unspeakable joy!

Heaven's maestro tapped his stand and a million angels began to sing their heavenly Hosannas that Jesus Christ is the Lord of death. And all the hallelujahs I ever knew joined hands and began their dance of joy about the cockles of my heart.

In that moment, in the only way God has of letting us know in advance, I knew it in my heart with a finality that nothing could ever shake from here on in, and I knew it for sure . . . *life lasts!*

And you can know it, too! For things are not as good as you thought, they're better! Much, much better! How much better, we have no way of knowing. We could not absorb it, even if we were told.

But we know now that when we approach the homeland, there will be lights and music, joy and laughter!

And the blahs will be gone . . . *forever!*